The BEGINNER'S Guide to BOWLS

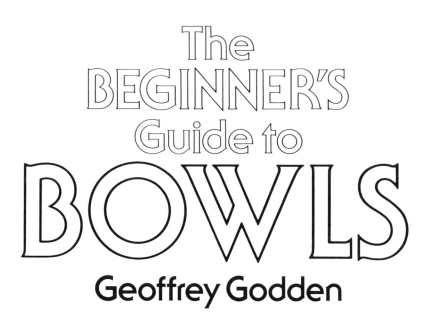

The BEGINNER'S Guide to BOWLS

Geoffrey Godden

Foreword by Tony Allcock

Macdonald
Queen Anne Press

A Queen Anne Press BOOK

© Geoffrey Godden 1988

First published in Great Britain in 1988 by
Queen Anne Press, a division of
Macdonald & Co (Publishers) Ltd
3rd Floor
Greater London House
Hampstead Road
London
NW1 7QX

A member of Maxwell Pergamon Publishing Corporation plc

British Library Cataloguing in Publication Data

Godden, Geoffrey A.
    The Beginner's Guide to Bowls.
    1. Bowling on the green.
    I. Title
    796.31   GV909

    ISBN 0-356-15112-3

Typeset by Cylinder Typesetting, London
Printed and bound in Great Britain at The Bath Press, Avon

Contents

Foreword by Tony Allcock

I have a friend whose intellectual ability I've always admired. Despite this gift he often misses out on the simple things in life, and finds difficulty in coping with them. It was not until early in 1988 that I had to study in-depth the apparently complicated action of delivering a bowl. Step by step, I identified the stages and, by keeping my study on a basic level, learned more about the action in one hour than I had in 32 years!

This book is written from the point of view of someone who, during the first few years of playing the game, has recorded his own personal experiences. The author has gone through the various aspects of the game of bowls from a raw and unadulterated standpoint. I can identify some of the problems experienced by the author when throwing his first bowl. For me, turning back the clock to the days when I began to play produces a fuzzy picture. This book has unveiled that picture to me and will enable me to identify the problems, peculiarities and advantages of being a 'beginner'. I must stress that there are advantages in being a first-season player – knowledge is limited so you stick rigidly to what you have learned. It is when you start to exercise other new-found skills that you might encounter problems!

Experienced players may think that this book will not help them. How wrong can they be! Stepping back and reviewing the basics is most refreshing and bowlers will know that this is a game that no one has finished learning.

Being interested in antiques, I happen to know about Geoffrey Godden's expertise in porcelain. Most dealers consider his book to be the 'bible' in this field. When people have read his bowls guide I am sure they will refer to it with the same frequency.

As bowlers progress and their skill improves they will change their personal philosophy of the game of bowls. However, I do feel that the new player in particular will identify with all that has been written and that this book will help and encourage the bowler to continue with this sport, which gives so much pleasure to millions of people.

Introduction

The aim of this book is to ease the would-be bowls player into a wonderful new world – to enable him or her, young or old, to gain the fullest benefit from this game of bowls – a sport open to the whole family.

I write this explanation of my ideals not as a veteran player but as one who has just ended his very first season as a budding, very amateur bowler. I survived and thoroughly enjoyed the experience even though, in the all too short season, I made every conceivable mistake known to man!

Believing in the truism 'a wise man learns by his mistakes', or rather in the more important follow-up 'but a genius learns by other people's mistakes', it occurred to me that as a raw beginner I was well placed to write an alternative introduction to this increasingly popular sport. Perhaps I am more fitted for this particular task than a respected veteran who has spent most of his life on the greens but has forgotten what it feels like to take the first tentative steps.

A non-bowler will also benefit from this introduction: an understanding of the game will enhance your enjoyment and appreciation if you like to watch games as you walk around our parks, or see the experts pitting their skill against each other on the television screen in the comfort of your home.

Note that I have not claimed to make you an expert or a world champion – that is an honour which comes to very few of us. However, we can all benefit from the game and share in the pleasure and relaxation arising from a basic understanding of its rules and subtleties. This book is addressed not to the few but to the many. Bowls is no longer the province of the retired male, but is increasingly popular among both sexes, young and old.

The experiences of my first year as a bowler are, of course, unique and personal, but the resulting advice I am endeavouring to pass on has been checked by others. It is not a case of the blind leading the blind, rather the enthusiastic amateur guided by accomplished authorities passing on their joint experience and knowledge.

Acknowledgements

This section should by rights be extremely long, for all those I have met on the bowling greens have been, without exception, extremely kind and helpful to me as an obviously new player. Constructive advice has come from all quarters: from experienced world-class players and from relative newcomers to the game anxious to pass on their new-found knowledge to the struggling novice. All these people had no idea that I was to write a book about my experience – indeed neither had I. I was merely treated to the traditional goodwill that all new bowlers will enjoy.

It would be wrong for me to single out by name those that have been especially helpful, so my belated thanks are here offered to all officers and members of the Worthing Bowling Club at Beach House Park, and to those of the Worthing Indoor Bowling Club at Field Place – the latter being the winter meeting place of bowlers from many West Sussex clubs.

I must however record my special thanks to the following cross-section of highly-qualified bowlers, who not only kindly agreed to my surprise request to look through the manuscript, but also thoroughly checked both my account and my views.

First Roy Downing, Britain's No1 Professional Bowls Coach. Roy gave me my first vital instruction in May 1985. All through the summer he gave tuition to those seeking to improve their game. He is an experienced and professional coach who has helped both novices and leading international players alike. It was Roy who took me and other new members of our club in hand, and taught me the essential basic points: grip; stance; delivery. His sergeant-major-like cry of, 'don't be a fairy', as my hands swung out in what I took to be an elegant fashion will always remain with me. Later I joined one of Roy's coaching courses and later still, when he had opened his specialist bowls equipment shop, he kitted out my wife Jean and our son Jonathan. Yes, I owe a very great deal to Roy Downing's professional advice. Likewise, my wife and I gained valuable help from Bill Shipton's course for beginners at Bournemouth.

Second, Lauri West, who was a great encouragement and help to me during my first year. Lauri is an accredited umpire and has a vast knowledge of the game, spanning some 50 years. You may have seen him umpiring the Gateway Masters Tournament.

Third, local bowls VIP Rex Glover-Phillips, who was president of the English Indoor Bowling Association 1974–75. Rex currently represents that association on the executive of the governing body, the English Bowls Council, of which he is a past chairman. He is also an England selector for both our outdoor and indoor teams.

Furthermore, I have had the cheek to ask Norman King, the former England player and World Champion Gold Medallist, author of that excellent book *Tackle Bowls this Way* and co-author with James Medlycott of *The Game of Bowls* , to check my views.

Further help has been offered by Peter Leask, the secretary of Worthing Indoor Bowling Greens Ltd, who checked the chapter on indoor bowling and by Chris Mills, the editor of *Bowls International* , who checked the section relating to my experience of the short-mat game. In this respect I wish to extend my thanks to Messrs Butlins and A.J. Aspin, the Southern General Manager and to Harry Lockett, the secretary of the English Short-Mat Bowling Association and Jim Rose of Bury Cooper Whitehead Ltd, the manufacturer of the *Regalgrene* indoor greens.

My son Jonathan agreed to read the text to see whether he, as a teenager and as yet a non-player, could understand the instructions or suggest any aspects of the game which in his view I had neglected to explain. Jonathan has also materially helped in our photographic sessions which illustrate this book.

Jeff Barnard of the Worthing Borough Amenities Department has also supplied illustrations, as has Peter Fleming. My thanks are also due to Reg Caldicott FIL, AM, MTS, the now retired Borough Amenities Officer and the various members of staff at Beach House Park.

Lastly on a very personal note, my gratitude is acknowledged to the typists; Janet Belton and Rosemary Manley; and to Gerald Dupernex for much valuable help. To my wife Jean, my thanks for not objecting too strongly to my great involvement in this new interest. You must see that I don't become totally addicted!

With the kind co-operation of these advisers I feel very confident that the information and advice given here is accurate, helpful and reasonably complete within the confines of a guide for beginners.

I can now only hope that you will derive as much enjoyment and healthy benefit from your bowls as I have. Being forewarned by my errors you can now be forearmed to avoid those initial blunders.

Geoffrey Godden
Worthing
West Sussex
July 1988

In the Beginning:
A Very Basic Guide

My bowling career started at 6.30 pm on Wednesday, 8 May 1985, when I was three months into my 56th year. This happened to be 82 years to the day after the English Bowling Association was founded with Dr W.G. Grace (of cricket fame) as the first president and moving spirit.

I write this account of my first season of outdoor Lawn Bowling in the belief that my experience as a rookie may be of help to others who are thinking of taking up this popular, leisurely and gentlemanly sport. Let me quickly explain that by 'gentlemanly' I mean mannerly, well-behaved, courteous, polite and civilised. When in this book I write of gentlemen, bowlers and players, I do not intend to differentiate between the sexes, both are equal so far as I and the game of bowls are concerned. As I shall be writing of my personal experiences I will be using the male gender, but naturally my advice applies to both men and women.

The ladies, by the way, are often more dedicated than their partners. The story about the lady in the front row of the closely-packed stand watching the Gateway Masters tournament at Worthing has a ring of truth to it. As the only vacant seat was next to her, the gentleman behind couldn't help enquiring if anybody was going to take the coveted front row place. 'Oh no,' replied the lady, 'that is my husband's seat and he died.' 'But,' said the man, 'aren't any of your friends going to use his seat?' 'Oh no,' she replied, 'they are all attending his funeral'!

Seriously, it is quite a daunting step to take up a new sport, especially in middle age, and find yourself in strange surroundings among folk you may not know and not properly equipped to play. I trust that this introductory book will lessen the shock and perhaps encourage those who have not yet taken the plunge to adopt this great and ancient game. You may note that in a quite important tournament, worth £3,000 in prize-money, an England player was partnered by a ten-year-old boy and a 76-year-old veteran. This strange combination did remarkably well!

As a beginner I must first admit to a certain amount of luck. I was born and brought up in a town very well provided with bowling greens and one which in recent years has become a centre of the bowling world – indeed it may well develop into the 'bowls capital' of England, with the World Bowls Championship due to be played here in 1992. I write of Worthing (or 'Sunny Worthing' as we love to call it), a town well situated on the coast some 60 miles south of London. As you will discover, this personal account takes place largely in Worthing and the illustrations often depict local greens. The game

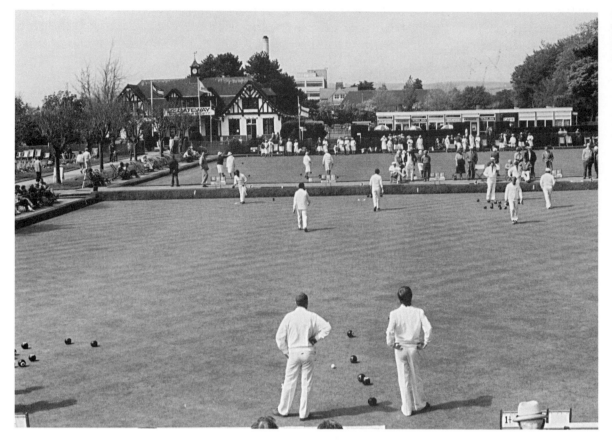

Beach House Park, Worthing. The 'Gateway Masters' is in progress on the championship 'C' green, while club games are taking place on 'B' green.

of bowls is, however, very much an international one and my bowls life in Worthing is mirrored in most towns in the British Isles and in Australia, New Zealand, South Africa, North America and many other countries.

Worthing has several bowling clubs. The senior one – the Worthing Bowling Club – was founded in 1909. Indeed, the Beach House Park plays host to six separate clubs, four for men and two for women, and there are four clubrooms. Usually the men and the women play their own matches but some mixed games are played and enjoyed by all. This large and beautiful park and its greens also act as the classroom of a professional bowls coach, Roy Downing, about whom I shall be writing later. The new headquarters of the English Bowling Association is also within the park complex.

The Worthing-based Gateway Building Society has for several years sponsored the Gateway Masters tournament (formerly the Kodak Masters), the highlights of which are featured on BBC television in the programme *Jack High*. The British Isles and the Home Counties International competitions as well as the World Championships have been staged in Beach House Park, where I roamed and played hide-and-seek when I was a young child.

It was the televising of the Gateway Masters that recently awoke my latent interest in bowls. I could no longer play rugger or badminton, the days of trying to play cricket with my son Jonathan had been left behind and my interest in sea-fishing had also waned. Here at last was a gentlemanly game which would suit me. No great or lengthy preparation seemed to be needed before the game started while each mini-game was quite short and did not call for any undue strength or prior exercise. The beautiful greens were readily accessible from home – paid for by my rate-paying grandfather and father. It looked so easy – one merely aimed a black ball at a smaller white one!

This was the game for me to ease into as my thoughts turned to retirement. A form of relaxation that would enable me to enjoy a certain amount of exercise in the fresh air and sunshine. A game to which I could perhaps introduce my family.

At the beginning of this chapter I claimed that my bowling career had started as I strolled into the clubroom on 8 May 1985, but it must now be admitted that I had earlier taken part in a single evening fun-game between our three local Rotary Clubs in August 1983. I enjoyed these short games where the scores were happily of little consequence, although I might have gained even more pleasure and satisfaction had I known a little more about the basic rules and method of play.

Very many would-be club players are introduced to the game by means of a casual, perhaps evening, game with a few friends, yet strangely no book that I have seen offers a single word of advice to such folk. Because the bowling bug has often been hatched at such informal 'roll-ups', it would perhaps be beneficial here if I define and explain the main points relating to the playing area and the basic equipment needed. The following describes the basis of the Flat Green game, as it is played in Britain, which is quite different to the Crown Green version, played mainly in the Midlands and Northern counties. Nevertheless, the essential skill is much the same as is evidenced by the fact that at least one Crown Green player has beaten the leading Lawn Bowls players in important championships. There is scope for much interplay between the two basic types of game.

The green is the main, large recessed area of grass with sides which can range between 33 and 44 yards in length, 42 yards being the norm. This is usually square in order to permit the direction of play to be changed by the green-keeper with the object of equalising wear; but if there are local restrictions it need not be square.

The grassed area is surrounded on modern greens by the ditch – the sunken gully some eight to 15 inches wide which is footed with gravel, pebbles or another similar substance to retain the position of a ditched jack or bowl. The sunken surface of pebbles, which can be between two and eight inches below the level of the playing surface, is surrounded by a raised bank of at least nine inches in height. Notice that on this raised bank there will be two white pegs or discs. These indicate a clear distance of 27 yards down the line of play from the near ditch. These markers are useful in determining that the delivered and centred jack has travelled 25 yards from the front edge of the mat. Obviously one has to take into account how far the mat has been moved forward from its initial placing, but the side bank-markers show the correct 25 yards when the front edge is six feet forward from the ditch. The near mark indicates the distance when playing from the opposite end of the rink.

If the new player comes across terms that are unclear, he should refer to the section headed 'Glossary of Terms' (page 147).

I have described the ditch and raised bank as being part of 'modern' greens because I find, much to my surprise, that as late as the First World War period some local greens boasted neither feature. An old photograph shows the green to be completely flat and the bowlers seem to be playing a game of Flat Green Bowls (or a version of the Federation game) without mats, dressed in the everyday clothes of the period.

Today each green displays a reference letter and its playing surface is further divided into 'rinks' – usually six to a green, although I understand that some clubs boast indoor greens with eight or more rinks. Rinks can vary in size but they are usually the

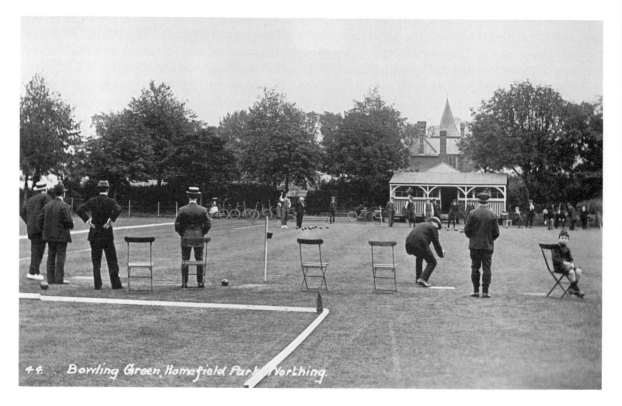

A Worthing Bowling Green as it was before the 1914-1918 War. Seemingly no ditch or banks were used, only wood surrounds similar to those used today in the indoor Short-Mat game.

maximum 19 feet in width, although the English Indoor Bowling Association allows rinks to be between 12 and 19 feet wide. The World Indoor Bowls Council permits rinks of between 15 and 19 feet in width. The limits of the rink are defined by corner pegs or markers in the bank. Between these is fixed (on prepared greens in Great Britain) a line of taut green thread lying along the surface of the grass. Each rink is therefore surrounded by a ditch and bank at each end and by a line of taut thread or string at the long sides – although there is a school of thought that would do away with the strings, as is the case in Australia and New Zealand.

Each game is played within this narrow strip. It is normal for each rink to be numbered so that the individual players or teams may then be allocated the rink they are to use, for example A1 – this meaning the first green and the first rink within it.

The centre point at the end of each rink will also be marked to enable the player to centre both the mat and the delivered (or placed) jack. Centring is obligatory, but the position of the mat and the jack on the central line is a matter of some choice.

The mat is normally of rubber or a like material. It has two basic and essential functions, but its positioning can also be used to great advantage by the thinking player because it may be moved before the commencement of the next 'end'. The mat helps preserve the surface of the green from the foot action of the players and to mark the area from which each bowler must stand to deliver his bowl during the progress of any one end. Each player must have at least one foot completely on – or over – the mat as he delivers the jack or his bowl.

The mat must be the regulation size, measuring 24 inches long by 14 inches wide. The

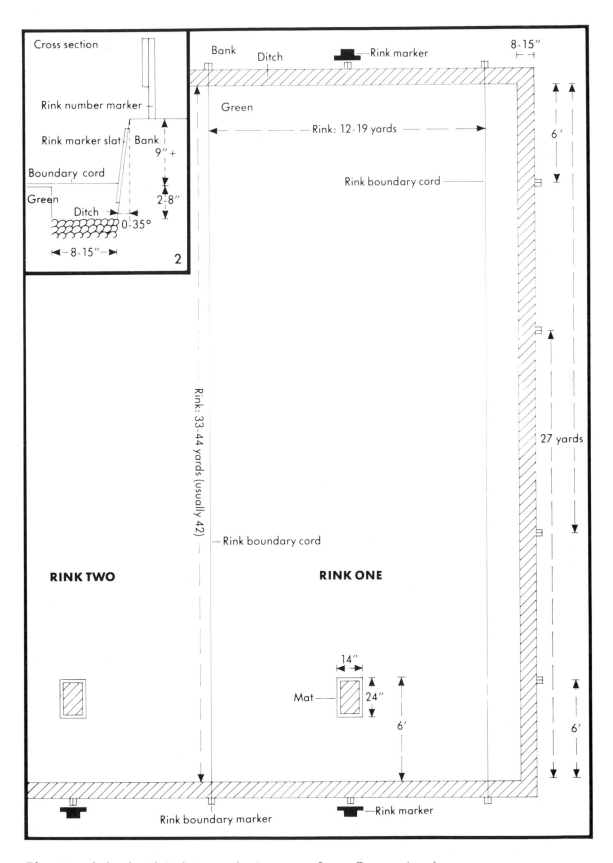

Cross section

Rink number marker

Rink marker slat

Boundary cord

Green

Ditch

8-15"

Bank

9" +

2-8"

0-35°

2

Bank

Ditch

Rink marker

Green

Rink: 12-19 yards

Rink boundary cord

8-15"

6'

27 yards

Rink: 33-44 yards (usually 42)

Rink boundary cord

RINK TWO

RINK ONE

14"

Mat

24"

6'

6'

Rink boundary marker

Rink marker

Plan view of a bowls rink (indoor or outdoor).   Inset. *Cross-section of a green.*

mat has a slightly ribbed, non-slip surface and is usually (in Britain) black with a white two-inch border. It is not necessary for the individual player to purchase his own mat, as it will be supplied by the club or by the green-keeper. I write in the singular but in practice two mats will be required, one for each end of the rink, because the game is played first one way and then back again in the opposite direction, thus each game is termed an 'end'.

No doubt every reader will know that the jack is the smaller white ball which is cast up the rink to serve as a target for the following bowls. This jack, to abide by the regulations for the outdoor game, will weigh between eight and ten ounces and have a diameter of between $2^{15}/_{32}$ and $2^{17}/_{32}$ of an inch, or 63 and 64 mm. Like mats, the jack is normally supplied by the club or green-keeper, but if you are going to practise alone it is advantageous to have your own. The jack used on most indoor rinks is much heavier than the regulation outdoor one.

The playing bowls themselves are made in matching sets of fours (although they can be used in twos, threes or fours), and will have a circumference of rather less than $16\frac{1}{2}$ inches (or a diameter ranging between $4^5/_8$ for size 0 and $5^1/_8$ inches for size 7, the largest permitted) and will weigh up to $3\frac{1}{2}$ pounds. I cannot be exact here as they are made to slightly different individual sizes and weights. There are also special bowls for the indoor game, although these are not essential.

The bowl can also be made of various materials. The old ones were of wood (traditionally *lignum vitae*) from which was derived the generic name 'woods' which is still used today. Nowadays most bowls are made of a plastic composition (often

Two matching bowls with the white jack. The bias side of the bowl (right) has the smaller central disc which, when held in the delivery hand, must be on the inside, nearest to the jack.

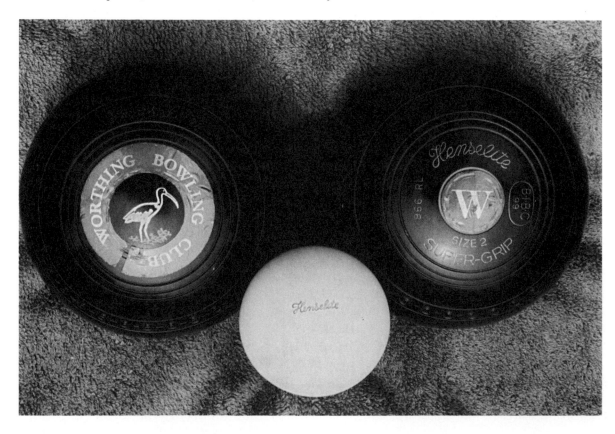

abbreviated to 'compo'). Remember, when purchasing a set of bowls, to ensure that they bear the official IBB (International Bowling Board) or BIBC (British Isles Bowls Council) stamp, showing that they have been tested.

Bowls are most certainly not balls! Cunningly, they are not exactly round but are, after moulding, cut or turned to make the running surface slightly lop–sided, giving the delivered bowl a slightly curving line – the all-important 'bias'. This bias will act in different ways depending on the bowls, the playing surfaces, the weather conditions, the speed of delivery and so on. It can even be affected by the position of the sun. It is almost as if each bowl has a will of its own! It is this bias, however, which makes the game unique and so challenging.

The equipment required by the beginner comprises a set of four bowls, which can usually be rented from the green-keeper's office. Before long you will need to buy your own set of bowls, which can often be purchased second-hand, but do not rush the purchase of your set until you are quite sure of the size that will suit you best. More information on the playing bowls is given in Chapter 9. You will not need your own jack or mat at this stage.

Club subscriptions do not include the free use of municipal greens: you will have to pay separately for their use either each time you play or by the purchase of a season ticket. The basic subscription will also probably not include the use of a locker within the club, but it is well worth the investment and will save much carrying of equipment to and from your home. It is as well to check in advance that rinks have not been pre-booked by others, that an important match or tournament is not in progress or that the greens are not unavailable for any other reason. Remember also that greens will only be in use between certain hours, as they have to be cut and otherwise prepared, and that the available time will probably be divided into fixed sessions – our greens are closed between 1.00 and 2.00 pm. It is also likely that they will not be open in the evening during the autumn if sunset is used as a criterion. In Britain, outdoor greens are usually available only during the five summer months.

You need no special equipment or dress to enjoy a game of bowls on your local municipal green as all can be rented on the spot for the required period. You will, however, need to know the basic essential points and have some knowledge of green etiquette. The question of good manners is very important for you will usually be sharing the green with other sets of players, all of whom are trying to concentrate on their play, and whose games are being carried on only a few yards from yours. The game of bowls is enhanced by the good manners associated with it and in this respect it can be compared with snooker or billiards.

When you establish the whereabouts of a local green check that it is municipal and not private, in other words that you will be permitted to use the facilities. You should also enquire whether bowls can be hired and, equally important, if special overshoes, slippers or other accepted footwear is available. You will not be permitted on the greens in ordinary shoes with a heel. Some green-keepers may allow reasonably flat-soled shoes but do not take this for granted. Ideally, you should have special bowlers' shoes with completely flat soles. Such shoes are discussed in more detail in Chapter 9. It would be as well to have with you a white cloth or duster so that you can clean or dry the bowls at intervals. This is often necessary before each delivery if the grass is damp.

So do your groundwork: check that a rink will be available, make an effort to visit the park, find the office, read the regulations and note the charges. I suggest that you arrange for at least one member of the party to arrive early. Delegate him to see the green-keeper, pay the dues, collect the equipment and any sets of bowls you may require (unless the players wish to choose them themselves to suit their own preference for size, weight or bias).

An evening's bowling is not going to be free of cost, and you should make the most of the available time which will prove all too short. Arrive early and be prepared to get on the rink as soon as it is available. It will save your valuable rink-time if you have decided in advance how you are going to play. Sort your teams or sides out; who is to act as skip or as lead? I have seen parties turn up and then spend half an hour of their session sorting out equipment, who is to play with whom and such matters that should have been resolved well before their paid-for time started to run away.

I have just written about teams and sides, for bowls is a competitive game. Bear in mind that you should have an even number of players for a convenient game. You can play singles (one against one); pairs (two teams of two); triples (two teams of three); fours (with four players on each side, which is the normal club game). A maximum of eight players can be accommodated on one rink.

You can play an amended game with an odd number if necessary. If three people wish to play together in a casual game or to practise, it is very easy to bowl as you would in singles, keeping individual scores, or to divide up two against one, with the pair having to reach a target score double that of the single player.

There is another interesting unofficial way of playing a threesome. You begin in the usual manner and amend the scoring system so that the nearest bowl to the jack is awarded four points, the next nearest three, the next bowl two and the fourth one point. The next end is then played by the bowlers delivering in the order of their last score – 4,3,2,1. I understand that some clubs even play competitions using this method.

I assume now that you are all present and properly equipped by the green and ready to play. Do you have two rubber mats and the jack? Have you each a set of bowls and flat-soled shoes? Have you found your rink? Leave your coats, jackets and odds and ends well clear of the bank surrounding the green, certainly not on the grassed area. As you step down on to the rink and later stand around, do be very careful to avoid stepping on and spoiling the crisp edge of the sunken ditch. Treat the grassed area with the greatest respect, as a precious Persian carpet. All that you should have on the rink are the rubber mat, the jack and your bowls. Make sure that you *place* the heavy bowls on the grass – never drop them. Having previously agreed the form of play and the order in which you are to bowl, you are ready to toss a coin for the first 'end'. I should mention at this point that in serious games you are given two trial ends, one each way, before the game proper is commenced. This is to allow both teams – one of which may be away from home – to gauge the speed of the green, to assess the grass-line to be taken and to test the playing conditions in general. By mutual agreement, this may be restricted to, say, two bowls each way, one forehand and one backhand. You can, however, request the full number of bowls for each of the trial ends.

The first player now needs to place the mat on the green. For the first end this is placed in the prescribed position: at a central point on the rink with the front edge of the mat six feet from the front of the ditch. As the mat is 24 inches long and is always placed lengthways, the back edge will be four feet from the ditch. This distance can be conveniently measured by turning the mat over on its length twice. The mat should be face-side-up with the criss-cross markings on the underside. Check that it is lined up on

Above right. *The mat. The easy way of measuring the six foot distance is to place it two mat-lengths from the ditch.*

Right. *The correct signal that the delivered jack should be moved to the left to lie centrally.*

Far right. *The jack is now central so raise your hand straight above the head, standing central on the mat.*

the central rink-markers and is straight. Any required measuring must take place after the jack has been centred. From this mat, which can be straightened but not otherwise moved, all deliveries are made.

The jack is now cast up the rink to serve as the target. In normal games this is delivered by the starting player, but for the real novice I would suggest that the jack be placed about three-quarters of the way up the rink in the central position. This short-jack placing will give the new player much more room to place his bowls and will make it unnecessary for him to try to project his bowl right up the green – and probably into the end ditch where it will be out of play and 'dead'.

In normal games the centring of the jack is very important. It is carried out by the skip, or in singles by the marker, moving the jack one way or the other across the rink as indicated by the player who has delivered the jack. The player will be standing centrally on the mat lining the jack up with the central rink-marker on the far bank, signalling to the marker to move the jack to the right or left by holding out the appropriate arm parallel with the ground until it is centred, when the player raises his arm above his head. The person centring the jack should do this with his hand while he stands or crouches to one side, so as not to block the view to the rink-marker. He should not, as is so often seen, move the jack about with his foot. Nor must he move the jack up or down the rink, unless the jack lies less than six feet from the ditch, in which case it is moved out to this distance and then centred.

Now you can proceed to see how near to the jack you can rest the bowls. This you will find is not nearly as easy as you may have thought or as it appears on television. To begin with, the bowls do not run in a straight line. As I have said, they have a built-in bias which ensures that they curve at normal delivering speeds, the more so as their speed

Left. *Get into the habit of checking the bias mark. I will here be delivering a back-hand shot.*   Right. *Position of the bowl as you stand on the mat.*

decreases. This bias will vary between different sets of bowls, on differing surfaces, at various times of the day and so on. However, it is essential to know how your bowl will curve. After all, you wish it to turn towards the jack, not to wander off into the next rink! Each bowl is therefore marked to show which is the bias side. The engraved rings of smaller diameter on the side of the bowl denote the bias side. These smaller markings should always be on the inside so that the bowl will curve inwards. Always check the bias before delivering the bowl. From time to time you will see even experienced players waste a shot by neglecting to do this. As a beginner you could pre-mark the bias side of your bowls with a bright sticker to help you recognise it instantly.

The first player takes his stance on the mat, holding a bowl. Let me assume that you are a right-handed person and, at this stage, wish to bowl only a simple forehand delivery. I like to stand just behind the mat, at one corner, say the left-hand corner. You can then step naturally forward on to the front half of the mat with your right foot facing a quarter-way, about 45 degrees, to the right. Bring the left foot up to the right so that both feet are together (or nearly so) and facing with the rest of the body a quarter-right. You must not be facing directly to the front: you need to bowl away from the target jack, not straight towards it.

Now direct your eyes and your whole concentration at a given point; let us say, for the first delivery, at the marker on the far bank which shows the right-hand boundary of your rink. Raise the bowl up in front of you at waist height with your hand bent forward at the elbow but to the side of the body in line with your shoulder. Steady it with the fingers of the left hand over the bias marking – a good way to check that the bias is on the inside, nearest the position of the jack. If you like, picture the bowl as the front wheel of a car. For this forehand delivery it is your right-hand wheel. The outside of the bowl with the larger rings should be in the position of the hub-cap, the bias is like the brake-drum on the inside of the wheel and the running surface of the bowl can be likened to the tyre. Remember that as you turn further to the right in your car, the relative position of the wheel – the inside and the hub-cap – will remain constant.

However, once you change from the forehand delivery (facing to your right) to the backhand delivery (facing to your left), so you must change to consider the opposite front wheel of the car. The 'hub-cap' will still be on the outside and the smaller markings – the bias side – will be on the inside. By the way, although we use the terms 'forehand' and 'backhand', you will always deliver your bowl with the same hand, whichever one feels natural – unless of course you are ambidextrous! You should nevertheless make use of your other hand to hold the heavy bowl before you take up your stance. Do not stand around holding a bowl for long periods in your delivering hand.

Having checked that the bias side of the bowl is on the inside, release your steadying left hand so that the bowl is held only by the right, which is in front of you at about waist level with your hand bent forward towards the elbow.

The question of your grip on the bowl is important. There are three basic methods, and many personal variations. In basic terms, the bowl will rest on your cupped fingers, and the middle of it should face straight forward along the running line or, using the analogy of our car wheel, under the tyre parallel with the centre of the tread. The thumb will usually be on the right side of the bowl with the tip near the ring markings. If the bowl is the correct size for your hand measurement it should stay in the hand if you turn it upside down- but bowls are heavy objects, so watch that you do not drop them on your feet as they can cause a painful injury!

As to the delivery, still facing partly right and with your eyes on the right-hand boundary marker – not on the jack – let the weight of the bowl take your hand downwards and allow it to swing backwards, in a natural straight-armed pendulum fashion, and then forwards again in a *straight* line. It is the weight of the bowl that carries your hand back. Do not jerk it back – it should be a slow, even action. As you let your hand swing forward of its own accord (or slightly before if you prefer), take a normal step forward with the left foot and rest your left hand on the left knee. This is to assist your balance while the forward step adds to the momentum of the delivery. There is little need to impart any extra force or power. Any extra length required should be achieved by increasing the back-swing and not by extra push. Remember the forward step should be in line with your right-facing body and not straight down the rink. Do not over-reach yourself – the object of the step is to keep your body in balance as your arm comes forward, not to upset the balance by a lunge forward.

As your right hand swings forward, you will ground your bowl some eight to 12 inches in front of your left foot or some two and a half feet in front of your right foot. Note that I write 'ground your bowl', by which I mean ease it on to the grass from your hand which at that point will be only an inch or less from the grass. To do this you will obviously have to be slightly crouched or stooped at this point. You should not bump the bowl down on to the surface from above. Ease it, run it, bowl it along the grass – keep that car wheel on the road!

Having grounded the bowl you can and should continue your forward movement slightly by taking a few steps down the rink. This is more important on a slow green when more momentum is required. Many beginners tend to stand still on the mat and this is frowned upon by some coaches, although I tend to do this as I study the run of the bowl and the grass-line taken. I believe one can best note any required correction from the point where you will deliver the next wood – the mat! Certainly, however, you should follow through with your hand on the same delivery line. This follow-through is very important, but do not pull the arm across the body, and remember to keep your eye on the aiming point and your head down. The Laws of the Game also state that at the moment of delivery of the bowl on to the grass, at least one of your feet must be entirely within the confines of the mat or over it.

Your first effort is unlikely to end its run very near the target. If it rests to the left of a central line you will need to aim out further to the right with your next delivery. If it ends up to the right, then narrow your angle or 'grass-line' to an aiming point nearer the jack. Remember, however, that a narrow grass-line will need less momentum than a wide line as the bowl has less distance to travel.

Now you have only to find the correct length, bowls being concerned in its very basic form with *width* (direction) and *length*. If your first bowl ended short of the jack but on a central line, then take the same angle or grass-line, but with your bowl held rather higher in front of the body. This should increase the natural back-swing and hence the forward arc and momentum of the delivered bowl, thereby increasing its length. It will also help to take a rather longer step forward with your left foot. Try to avoid pushing the bowl forward for extra length – we should be concerned with the swing rather than the throw. Do remember to continue to swing your arm forward in a straight line – your follow-through.

Conversely, if your first shot over-runs the jack by a few yards, start with the bowl lower in front of your body to produce a shorter back-swing and a slower delivery. You can also adjust your forward step to a shorter one. Note that it is best to be too long and to adjust your length downwards in subsequent deliveries. The basic shot enabling your bowl to end up near, or touching, the jack is called the 'draw', giving rise to such expressions as 'just a simple draw' and 'draw to it'.

Left. *Correct step forward on to the mat facing about a quarter right.*

Right. *A well grounded bowl released just above the level of the grass.*

Having delivered your first bowl watch its forward delivery until it comes to rest. The time taken for its run will vary depending not just on the distance of the jack down the rink but also on the speed of the green, which can vary greatly. Make a mental note of any corrections that may have to be made in future deliveries. To help you in pairs, triples or fours, the skip (or captain) of each team positions himself at the far end of the rink behind the jack. From there he can signal to his player how far short or past the jack his bowl has rested. This is very often not at all clear to the bowler because of the length of the rink and the visual foreshortening involved. The skip will decide tactics and indicate the type of shot he requires. He will also mark 'touchers' and place 'dead' bowls on the bank. When it is the skip's turn to bowl, the other members cross over to stand behind the head.

Once your bowl has come to rest, your possession of the mat and the whole rink ceases and it becomes the turn of the next opposing player to take his place on the mat. You bowl only one wood at a time and delivery is taken in rotation. In singles you use all four bowls, the two contestants A and Z playing AZ, AZ, AZ, AZ. In pairs, the two teams A and Z will still use all four bowls which are delivered A1 Z1, A1 Z1, A1 Z1, A1 Z1 by the 'leads', to be followed by the skips; A2 Z2, A2 Z2, A2 Z2, A2 Z2. If six people are playing a triples game, each uses only three bowls in the order: lead, number two, skip. If eight are engaged in a fours, then each should use only two bowls, and the team will play lead, number two, number three and skip. The roles of each member are discussed in Chapter 3.

Once all the players have delivered their bowls the end has been completed. Place the mat flat on the top of the bank (not over-hanging the edge) and walk up to the head – the name given to the closely packed (one hopes) group of bowls resting at the jack end – to determine the score. One point is awarded for the bowl nearest to the jack and additional points are given for each further bowl of that player or team until the score is stopped by a nearer bowl from the opposition. In a singles match one can score none, one, two, three or four points, but only one player or side can score in each end. Do not move the bowls until the score has been mutually agreed. It is the job of the player conceding his opponent's shot to remove these scoring bowls. Keep a tally of your score – it is preferable to write it down, although a useful dodge for casual games is to use pebbles taken from the ditch and placed on the bank to record the score.

As you progress to play in more serious games you will need a bowler's measure to check which bowl is lying 'shot', i.e. which is nearer the jack and therefore scoring. You will also need a piece of chalk to mark 'touchers'. These are bowls which have touched the jack during their original delivery. Such touchers have no special scoring significance, but if delivered or later pushed into the ditch they remain 'live' and can therefore be counted in a score provided that no opposing bowl is nearer the jack. Remember to wipe off old chalk marks.

Other bowls delivered or later moved into the ditch are 'dead' and cannot be considered in a score, as is a bowl that lies entirely outside the side boundaries. A jack hit out of the rink is also dead and the end is replayed. However, the game continues if the jack is hit or trailed into the ditch after it has originally been correctly delivered. Dead bowls should be removed from the ditch at once and placed out of the way on the bank.

Once you have agreed the score you start the next end by playing in the reverse direction back down the rink. The player or lead of a side who won the previous end now has the privilege of placing the mat and casting the jack as well as delivering the first bowl. Ideally, a mat should be available at each end of the rink but, if you have only one, then you will have to move it from end to end as the game progresses.

These leading privileges can be very important, especially as one progresses to play in more serious games, as the leading player has the advantage of placing the mat at his discretion, preferably in consultation with his skip, within the confines of the regulations (not less than four feet from the ditch and the front edge not less than 27 yards from the front ditch). Still, this gives you about 12 yards to play with. You can therefore place your mat to suit your own game: well forward if you prefer to bowl short lengths; well back if you do better with a long delivery – taking into consideration the length fancied by your opponent. Play to your likes, not his!

You can also cast the jack to your preferred length – short, medium or long. If you over-run it into the ditch or fail to deliver it to the minimum 25 yards from the front of the mat the opposing player has the chance to reposition the mat to his liking and to deliver the jack to his preferred length, although the leading position does not change. Speaking of positions, remember that the rules do not permit any change of the bowling order once this has been agreed and the game started. A lead will always go first, the skip last, and they cannot change positions or duties. The exception arises in the Federation game where changes are permitted.

The score is normally carried on from one end to the next until one player or team reaches a predetermined total, say 21. A total score of 15 might be better if you are only playing for an hour or so but much depends on the different skills of the players. In a well-matched game the scoring may well proceed by one or two per end but, obviously, if one person or side is superior, their score will race ahead. Alternatively, one can play a

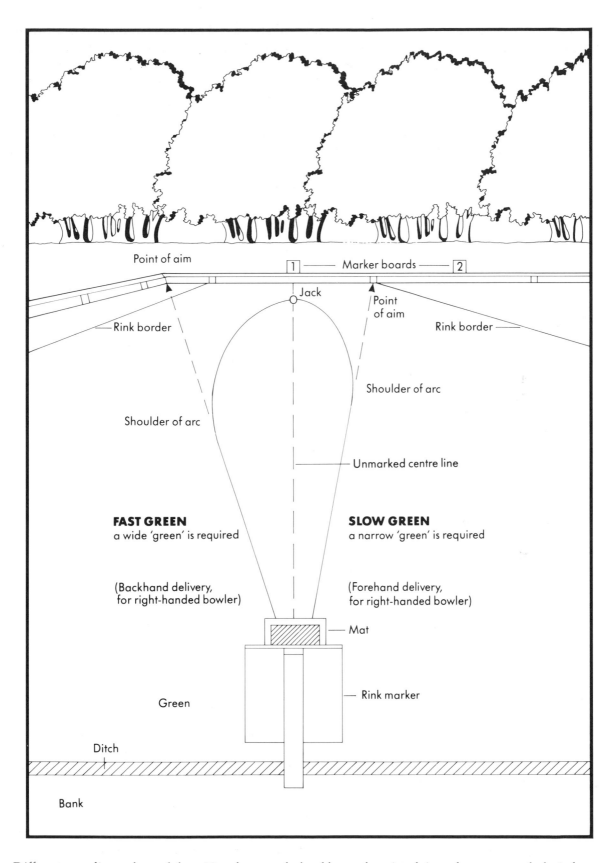

Different grass lines – fast and slow. Note the arc as the bowl leaves the point of aim and curves towards the jack.

predetermined number of ends, say 21. You can also score in sets as in tennis, but this is not an official mode of play. For an evening's play it would probably be better to pre-set a given time, the highest score at that hour denoting the winner. Once agreed, it is better not to vary the finishing time, although an extra end or two might perhaps be played for a round of drinks!

I have as yet confined my remarks to singles (which can also be played with three people), pairs, triples and fours, but you can devise various other tests of skill using the standard rink.

For example, lay a large white handkerchief on the grass in a central position some three-quarters of the way up the rink. Discover how difficult it is to rest your bowl on such a target. It is surprisingly difficult for a novice to land his bowl on an even larger area such as a spare rubber mat placed wrong-side up in a similar position.

You can also obtain a special circular rubber mat marked off in rings, like a shooting target, to play Target Bowls, which is suitable for both indoor and outdoor use. It is very much more difficult to rest your bowls near the centre of the target than you may think. If the jack is placed in the centre of the circular mat it may help to give the novice a better idea of distance.

Another practice routine is to place two jacks, one 12 or 18 inches or so in front of the other, three-quarters of the way down the rink. The object here is to project two bowls, using one forehand and one backhand delivery, through this gap from right to left and then from left to right, delivering from the mat. When you can achieve tricks like this you should be joining a club and playing serious games.

When you decide to take up the sport, contact an experienced player, a local club-member or a local sports dealer, one of whom should be able to guide you along the path to more advanced play and pleasure.

This very brief description should have enabled you to understand the fundamentals of the game so that you can plan and enjoy an amusing evening on the green. I trust that after a few such casual games you will wish to improve your technique and learn more about the game. To this end, I would advise you to read and acquaint yourself with the laws governing the various basic types of game (see Appendix 1). Read the rest of this and other instructional books, although you can leave for the time being those which seek to turn you into a world champion.

Try to seek out an experienced player who is prepared to play a few ends with you to iron out any basic errors. Most authorities advise you to practise, practise and practise, but this will not be beneficial if you are only consolidating errors. Perfect your delivery and then practise until it becomes second nature. I have been writing of outdoor summer bowls but most of my remarks apply equally to the indoor game, which is explained in Chapter 5.

Seek to join a local club, playing with other folk whom you will find most helpful. Do not be afraid to ask questions or seek advice. If you are serious, the services of a professional coach or a course of instruction will undoubtedly be well worth the expense. Bear in mind that it costs nothing to wander around a park watching games in progress. You can pick up many useful hints just by keeping an eye open. Note any aspects of play that are not clear to you and try to find the answers. The person sitting or standing next to you may be able and willing to explain.

Relax, have an enjoyable game and have fun.

A Club Member's Progress

I am now aware that there are two schools of thought on how the novice should be introduced to the game. The manner in which I was brought to the green is probably the one adopted by most clubs, but some learned authorities feel that this should be preceded by lectures or demonstrations. This approach was championed by the late R.T. Harrison of Australia in his excellent book *How to Become a Champion at Bowls*.

Mr Harrison described the experiences of most new players when he stated, 'He meets the members, and is invariably taken straight into the game. That is to say, he is encouraged in doing what he is most eager to do himself, viz go out on to the green . . . The first fatal lesson, or demonstration, is his undoing . . . That recruit thus joins the great army of 75 per cent, the ever-increasing number spoilt for all time in their toddling days . . .' This highly respected author expands his ideas at some length and I am certainly not in a strong position to argue with his views. Nevertheless, I fancy that most would-be bowlers will continue to be introduced to the game in the time-honoured way, that is by being taken on to the green to bowl trial woods without the benefit (or otherwise) of indoor tuition, lectures, demonstrations or films.

Maybe the novice has had the good sense to read a reliable book which has explained the rules, the basic methods of play and some of the traditions and customs. Yet the greater part of his learning will come from practical experience and from the help of established players. This is how David Bryant and most other players of international repute learned their initial technique before building upon such foundations.

My apprenticeship began thus. I have already mentioned Roy Downing, our local professional club coach, who runs a series of instructional courses on my local greens. I had met Roy through business and asked him how one entered for his courses. He explained that they offered advanced tuition for the experienced player and were not aimed at the beginner. He rightly suggested that I should first join a local club.

He offered to propose me as a member of Worthing Bowling Club. Much to my surprise, I found myself elected in a very short time and with a remarkably low subscription to pay. Later my son Jonathan was accepted while he was still at school – catch 'em young! I was advised that club roll-ups were held on Wednesday evenings and that Roy would be on hand to give advice and help to new members. Such help was much needed, for I had neglected to consult any of the books available on the sport.

From the moment I first entered the clubroom that Wednesday in May, 1985, I felt at home and among friends. The then vice-captain, Gerry Bridger, had been a class-mate of mine at school, while I knew by sight or reputation half the worthies gathered there to play bowls, and even past presidents and champion players, whose photographs were arranged around the walls, were well known to me. The great George (John) Scadgell, a former England skip, has a business less than 100 yards away from my own. Much of our furniture and our carpets were supplied by this bowls champion's family furnishing business, but could I follow in his bowling footsteps? Well, I could but try.

On the first club evening I arrived extremely ill-equipped. True, I had done a little homework and discovered that the accepted informal club dress was grey trousers and white shirt (plus a white pullover if necessary), preferably with a club tie. I had also bought a pair of special bowlers' shoes with flat soles and brown uppers. I was at least dressed correctly and could therefore feel reasonably at ease. But as to equipment, I had none.

The club captain introduced himself and hoped I would enjoy my time in the club. Almost as an afterthought he asked if I had a set of bowls and offered me his own when I admitted that I hadn't. Later I was to borrow his trousers, but that is another story! The set of bowls and the flat-soled shoes were the only equipment I needed then, the club supplying the rubber mat and white jack.

Having been loaned a set of bowls, I made my way with some dozen other club members to our allotted green. I can remember finding the four bowls surprisingly heavy and cumbersome. I envied the experienced players their carrying bags and resolved to make the purchase of one a priority. I was pleasantly surprised when we were all introduced to each other in a particularly friendly way, and we all shook hands. The friendliness was to be maintained on all future occasions.

Having put down mats the new players were treated to a discussion on the grip to be used in holding and delivering the bowl. There are three basic ways of holding the bowl – the 'cradle' grip, 'claw' grip and 'finger' grip – and which you employ is a matter of personal choice. It is a question of which feels the most natural or, as you progress, which results in the cleaner and more accurate delivery. This natural variation largely stems from the fact that hands and fingers are of different sizes. Furthermore, the bowls used may well be of different dimensions and weights. Also some bowlers will obviously be stronger and have better control than others.

You will later observe that some successful players use grips that are unique to them, but as a beginner it is best to take advice and adopt one of the established methods. Therefore, I recommend you to read about the three standard grips, study the relevant illustrations in this book and then spend some considerable time – over several bowling sessions – discovering which method suits you, your hand, your bowls and the type of delivery you find most successful and comfortable.

I was told by Roy Downing to pick up my bowl and hold it the way that came naturally to me. I happened to adopt the **cradle grip**, which seems to be the most popular in the British Isles, so I will describe it first.

If you do not have a bowl handy test the grip using a large grapefruit, which will reproduce the shape of a wood quite well but will be considerably lighter in weight. If you spin the grapefruit up in the air a foot or so and catch it, I think your initial hold and your catching action can be likened to the cradle grip. The fruit will have rested in the palm of the hand and your fingers will have spread slightly along the bottom and curled a short way up the front of the fruit, while your thumb will be on the right side (assuming that you are right-handed). This represents the cradle grip for a forehand delivery.

An important point to remember is that the fingers, particularly the middle finger, should point straight to the front (in practice most have their fingers at a slightly oblique

Above left. *The cradle grip seen from the side.*

Above right. *Front view of a cradle grip. The claw grip differs in that the bowl is slightly further forward in the hand and the thumb is higher, by the ring markings.*

Below left. *The finger grip with the bowl held well forward by the tips of the fingers.*

angle). If your bowls are not too big for you, it should be possible to retain one in this grip when turning your hand and bowl to an upside-down position.

The thumb should be used only to steady the wood in the palm prior to delivery; it should not grip the side, certainly not at the moment the bowl is rolled forward from your hand on to the grass or carpet. Remember also that your fingers should be parallel and facing straight forward not spread out at various angles. Your little finger should not creep up the bias side of the bowl which will cause it to wobble. To obviate this tendency you can move your fingers slightly off-centre towards the outside, closer to the thumb.

When you held the grapefruit and tossed it in the air, you may well have naturally imparted a forward spin to the fruit, which would have kept the object on an even, unwobbly path. As you deliver the bowl you will also impart a forward spin which will materially help its running action and increase the length it will travel for a given amount of momentum.

The **claw grip** is a popular variation of the cradle. Here the two middle fingers are kept close together, while the first and fourth fingers are more widely spread, creeping up the side of the bowl. The thumb is cocked up high over the bowl approximately along the larger cut rings running around the wood. The fingers and thumb act like claws giving a widespread grip, so the bowl is placed rather more forward in the hand than would be the case in the cradle grip. This grip is suitable for most conditions, on slow or fastish greens, as long as your bowl is the correct size for your hand.

For the **finger grip** the bowl is placed well forward out of the palm of the hand on to the spread fingers, with the thumb reaching towards the top as in the claw grip. Some players favour keeping the fingers close together, not spread.

The finger grip is probably the best on very fast rinks where little power is required. Some bowlers are of the opinion that they can achieve a more delicate touch and more precise control with the forward placing of the bowl on the fingers, but I fancy that few, if any, coaches would suggest that the new player using British outdoor greens should at first adopt this grip.

The several books by Australian players tend to advocate the finger grip because it suits their fast surfaces. R.T. Harrison is particularly against the cradle grip: 'Players who palm the bowl are all more or less dumpers'. He places great emphasis on the power of the thumb, which is admittedly little used in the cradle grip, except to steady the wood.

David Bryant's book is also very helpful on the question of the basic grips. Experiment if you like, but settle on the grip which seems the most comfortable to you and which gets the most consistently good results. While David Bryant greatly favours the claw, others would not change from the cradle or from their slight individual variation. Look around you at other players on the green; there are a multitude of styles – some good, some not so good. The grip you want should be comfortable and firm, but not tight; one that will enable you to deliver the bowl in a well-controlled manner time after time.

Having agreed my grip on that first evening, and explained to me about bias, Roy invited me to try my luck at delivering my first bowl. Full of confidence, I took up my stance on the mat facing the centred jack. I was careful to keep my eye on the jack, which I incorrectly took to be my point of aim. I swung my arm forward and thump went the bowl as I all but fell over on my face! The bowl ended up in the ditch well to the left of the jack. At least my bias was on the correct side – perhaps one point out of ten for my first delivery? I had in 15 seconds made almost every mistake in the novice's book. Let us examine these silly but all too common errors.

Firstly, my stance on the mat. My first two serious errors were to face the jack and to keep my eye on the jack as a target. I would have been well-positioned if I had been aiming a gun or bowling with a circular ball, but I failed to take into account the bias. For about the first three-fifths of its course, the bowl moves along almost in a straight line. It then begins to curve markedly as the speed of the bowl decreases; the action of the bias becoming progressively more pronounced as the bowl slows down, sometimes even turning it round to bring it back towards the mat in its last few inches of 'trickle'!

The degree of bias depends on many varying factors. As I explained in Chapter 1, not only must we consider that different sets of bowls possess different degrees of bias (number 3 being the norm) but that the material of which the bowl is composed – and its condition – will affect its travel. Additionally, the surface on which it has to travel will greatly influence the effect. All outdoor rinks vary even between a forehand and a backhand delivery and according to the time of day or the weather conditions. To account for this, one should of course not aim at the jack, but rather at a point several yards to the right or the left. The bias of the bowl will then bring it back to the centre, provided that the delivery was correct and that the weight and length of the delivery were also well judged.

It thus follows that you do not face the front, rather your whole body should face the line that you judge to be the correct one.

Before delivering the bowl I like to have a practice swing of the arm, forward and back once or twice; not only to loosen up but to try to ensure that the swing is straight and that my arm is on target. Do not overdo such mock-deliveries, even though they have a calming influence and improve your aim. Also, do not have bulky objects in your right-hand pocket as these can impede a straight swing of the arm.

You will almost certainly not have happened upon the correct grass-line for your first delivery. However, as long as your delivery is sound and constant and you grass the bowl smoothly, there should be little difficulty in finding a reasonable line so that your woods come to rest in a central line with the jack – at least that is what we were told!

The question of finding the correct length to nestle up to the jack is rather more difficult. This is where experience, practice and a delicate touch come into play. I have already explained the basic method of lengthening or shortening the delivery, namely by increasing or decreasing the back-swing and speed of your delivery arm and of the step forward with your left foot. A higher back-swing is brought about by holding the bowl higher in front of the body, or conversely, lower, if you wish to deliver a shorter bowl. Many beginners seek to take a smaller angle of delivery for a short delivery – this is incorrect since the arc will remain constant.

Do not become despondent if, like me, you make a poor showing at your first attempt. This is quite natural and you are likely to be extremely erratic for a considerable period. The vital thing is to learn from your mistakes, to strive to overcome them and to get in as much practice as your other commitments permit.

Left. *The author making every beginner's error in one go: left hand thrown out to the side; foot partially off the mat; bowl canted; eyes looking down, not at the aiming-point; a bowl and duster in a distracting position.*

Right. *Good position for casting the jack, so that the arm swings along the central point.*

The new player should also learn how to cast the jack. A well-delivered jack will inspire confidence in the player and show the opposition that you are not the novice you appear to be. If you are playing in the lead position it will fall to you to deliver the jack should your side have won the toss or have been nominated to start by the other side, or if your own side has won the previous end.

Having laid the mat in the correct position (right way up!), stand on it with your feet facing forward but at the side, so that your delivery arm occupies the central position. Now hold the jack on the tips of your middle fingers with your thumb steadying it at the top. Swing your arm back and forth in a straight line, just as you would with a bowl. If your swing is straight the jack should travel down the rink and stop in a good central position requiring very little centring. If it is dead-centre you will feel uplifted and your opponent will be rather taken aback at your skill. He and you and your skip will be even more impressed if it rests not only centrally but at the required distance – at the skip's feet. Yet, with practice, this is what should happen nine times out of ten. I am always shocked at the number of times leading players deliver a jack into the ditch so forfeiting the opportunity of casting it to the other player or side.

In casting the jack you also have a chance to judge the speed of the green. If you are well-practised and your first jack runs a few yards past the required spot, then obviously the green is running faster than normal or faster than the green you have been used to. Obviously your bowls will also be affected, so you will need to take this into consideration when you deliver the woods. Also, if the unbiased jack should run in an untrue, erratic manner the surface is probably faulty at that point and will need watching. Thus, in more ways than one, the delivery of the jack can win or lose a game.

If you wish to find favour with your skip, I would suggest that you pay attention to the following oft-neglected points.

a) Look to the skip before you deliver each bowl. Is he also ready? Has he any instructions? Are you being asked to use a forehand or a backhand delivery? Does he want a simple draw to the jack or a bowl placed two yards to the rear? If no information is forthcoming, however, do not shout up for instructions – the skip may well wish to keep his plan or strategy to himself and not share it with the opposition.

b) Having delivered your bowl watch it right down to its final position. Now turn your attention to the skip to read any information he is signalling back. Acknowledge with a slight wave or raised hand that you have seen and understood his signal. Do not, as so many do, deliver your wood and then turn around to pick up your next. Your skip does not want to signal to your backside, nor can you observe any faults as to line or length. There is plenty of time to arm yourself with the next bowl. Furthermore, information should only be sought or given when you are in possession of the rink.

c) Try to keep your deliveries well up to the jack or past it. In most games the jack will be moved during play and it will be trailed or knocked backwards not towards you, so that a back wood can easily become the shot wood. Also short deliveries could well hamper the skip's own delivery-line when his turn comes to make a vital late shot. If you have to err, make sure it is on the long side.

d) It will be helpful to both yourself and the skip if you tell him in advance if you have any special weakness (or strength) – if you cannot reach a very long jack or manage a backhand shot, for example. He can then try not to embarrass you or call upon you to achieve the impossible. A word beforehand is better than a belated explanation or apology.

e) Remember to leave any in-play signalling or suggestions to the number three. The separate duties of each player are discussed later.

Match or More Advanced Play

In my first season I had no intention of partaking in matches. My sole aim was to see if I could play to a reasonable standard and not disgrace my name! I quickly decided that I was enjoying myself and that I could relax and forget my business worries. All I now wanted was to practise and have a few roll-ups with fellow club members.

However, those members kept asking if I had put my name down for matches. When I laughed and said that I was not good enough, I was quickly told that it was the best way to learn and to improve my game. Still, I could not bring myself to add my name to the match lists on the club noticeboard – I was simply afraid of letting the side down.

Then one Saturday evening the phone rang. The club captain asked if I could possibly play in a match the following Monday. He was in a fix as several members, including himself, would be away at a county match, so he was phoning around to try to get a full team together for a home club match. In desperation, I explained that I did not have the required white trousers. As quick as a flash he offered to supply a spare pair. I somewhat reluctantly agreed to fill in, quite forgetting that I had an important Rotary lunch on that day!

Needless to say, on this unique occasion, my first match, the lunch went on and on. I just had no chance to get away until well after 2.00 pm, still dressed for business, still far from the green, and unable to find a parking space when I did finally arrive. The result, as you will have realised, was that I arrived breathless and late on the green. This was the worst possible introduction to match play. I resolved there and then first, always to plan to be correctly dressed and on parade at least a quarter of an hour before the match, and second, not to attempt to play an important game directly on top of a Rotary lunch!

Worse was to come, for after the skip had finished glowering at his late rookie, he asked me for my match fee and tea-money. Now nobody had thought to mention such things to me and I was penniless! I have not yet finished my tale of woe. Having placed my sparkling new bowls on the green, somebody said 'but these aren't marked'. I was at a loss to know what he was talking about. It seemed that, when representing a club as I now was, your bowls had to have identifying stickers. Hurriedly, such labels bearing the legend 'Worthing Bowling Club' were produced from someone's bag and affixed to the side of my bowls. Very belatedly, I was ready.

I bowled my first match wood still slightly breathless, very embarrassed and regretting that moment when I had been talked into playing – especially as it had necessitated taking an afternoon off from my business for almost the first time in 40 years.

The home club usually lets visiting teams have first bowl rather than toss for the privilege. It therefore transpired that my opposite number, the visiting lead, took the mat first. As he made his delivery, I happened to turn to speak to someone standing behind me. I was immediately told off by our number three (standing in for the skip who was at the other end of the rink). 'You should be standing behind that player watching his line and delivery. Copy it or improve on his line, learn from him, size up his strengths and weaknesses, never *ever* turn around and chat. Concentrate at all times.'

This was extremely valuable advice and I now make a point of standing behind each bowler to observe his line and to learn the characteristics of the green. In a fours game, I bowl only twice per end, but I can learn from seven other players and their 14 deliveries. Remember, however, not to follow the good line of a left-handed player if you are right-handed, and also bear in mind that other bowls may not match yours for weight or bias.

I can't say that the bias was wrong on my first delivery, but further embarrassment came with my third bowl of the day. Traditionally, as the newest player I was lead (some clubs prefer to make such weak players number two), so I had to place the mat. Such a day it was that I managed to get it the wrong way up! Not that I knew, until corrected, that the mat had different top and bottom surfaces. The bottom on ours has criss-cross ribbing whereas the top has ribbing only across the narrow way.

I will spare you further details but, for the record, we won our match and once I had settled down I thoroughly enjoyed my afternoon. A few lucky deliveries enabled my skip almost to forgive my early errors. There was, however, one last embarrassment. Having completed our 21 ends, much to my surprise we commenced another end – a penny on the jack to raise funds for our charity box. Again, being totally unprepared, I had to borrow a penny! By the way these last 'penny ends' are normally played in reverse, ie skip first, lead last.

At the end of every game, make a point of shaking hands with all the other players and offering a few kind words to express your appreciation of an enjoyable, well-fought game. Thank your skip for a good game and for his understanding of your failings!

My colleagues had been quite right – one does learn from match play by striving to emulate better and more experienced players. I resolved to try another match, but to put my name down for a day and time that suited my other commitments. As a now committed match player I resolved to buy my own whites (ones that were a comfortable fit) and to have match fee and tea-money and some small change available in my bag.

My next home match was on a Saturday afternoon which suited me far better: bags of time for an early, light (non-Rotary) lunch; ample time to get washed and properly dressed in my whites; no rush to get to the park; adequate time to park the car and report to the clubhouse and my skip. I had money ready in my pocket for the match fee and tea, and I was much more at ease and had put in a considerable amount of practice since my last match – my bowls were now beginning to go where I wanted them rather than seeming to have a will of their own! It was a most beautiful September afternoon too.

As my wife rightly tells me, I look daft in a cap, so I thought it would be a rather bright idea to put some sun-cream on my face, especially on my nose which tends to peel in the sun. It is difficult to put such cream on one's face without getting it on the hands, so two minutes later, when I went to deliver my first bowl I could not pick it up! My creamy hands just slid off. It took a surprisingly long time before I could get rid of the last of the grease to be able to hold and control my bowl. You can in fact purchase proprietary preparations to improve your grip; beeswax is said to be good and, of course, your cloth is just as useful for drying your hands as it is for polishing the bowl. If you are a perfectionist, have a spare cloth for your hands but be warned that dye can come off new yellow or other coloured cloths and so spoil your new whites, especially in wet weather!

Once I could grip the bowl, I played quite well in that match. One weakness did, however, show up rather badly. As lead I had to cast the jack whenever we had won the previous end. My task was simply to deliver that jack to the length dictated by my skip who would come up the rink and stand at that required length. My jack was either too short or made the skip jump in the air as it went under his feet!

It is really more important for the lead to deliver a precise jack than it is to draw to it with his following bowls. If he fails to get a shot wood, other members of the team can rectify his error, but nobody can readily compensate for an incorrectly-cast jack, particularly one that is too long to suit your team.

Like most beginners I did not pay enough attention to the casting of the jack. For example, when I had a practice roll-up I used to bring along two jacks and place them on the green at the position to which I wished to bowl. This might have been convenient and quick, but my time would have been better spent casting the jack to various predetermined lengths. As with all aspects of the game, practice makes perfect.

I should also mention here that the lead should not alter the length of the jack or the position of his mat while his side is winning. The existing length obviously suits his team better than it pleases the opposition. Movement of the mat or jack is a ploy to be tried when one is losing.

While the skip will probably indicate the length of jack he requires, you will wreck his plans if you move the mat on your own initiative, thus affecting the length between the bowler and the jack. The lead should note carefully where he last placed the mat and repeat this placing until told otherwise by the skip or his deputy.

I must also admit that on a later occasion I got into dreadful trouble with the skip for doing this when we had lost end after end and were about 12-1 down. When my chance at last came, I moved the mat well forward from the back position that was favoured by the other team. I thought this was a good and accepted tactic, but it resulted in us losing that end by six shots. My short-mat ploy had put our team off more than it disrupted the play of the more experienced opposing side. My skip told me off in no uncertain terms for moving the mat position without his permission or instructions. He was quite right, although had we won that end by six points he might have congratulated me on my good sense! Skips are individuals; get to know their particular likes and dislikes.

Another error I made in my second match was similarly due to over-confidence. As lead, I now tended to butt in on the duties of others. On one end I queried the score, pointing out that my bowl should have been included. However, the count is the responsibility of the number three and other members should not interfere. Slightly later, while the skips were on the mat and the rest of us who had delivered our woods were grouped behind the head, I again erred. The opposing skip delivered his last bowl, which was a beauty, and turned our potential score of four into one down, leaving our skip to rectify the position with his final wood.

Our number three signalled two very difficult alternatives by which the skip might – if he was David Bryant – retrieve the situation. Just as number three finished his direction I remembered that I had a toucher in the ditch. This bowl was, of course, live so I excitedly shouted up to the skip, 'put the jack in the ditch!' This was quite good advice, but a word in the third's ear would have been the correct way of delivering it.

If the position at the head changes then a skip requires clear advice on the recommended line of action from his deputy, not conflicting suggestions from every member of his team! In this instance it might have been better for him to have left the mat and walked back up to view the head. He could then have seen the situation for himself and perhaps discussed the difficulties with his deputy. This is the practice that you see correctly adopted by the leading international players in their matches. It also enables the skip or team to keep their intended tactics to themselves.

A shouted instruction to 'put one at the back' is a clear signal to all that the last bowl is likely to be a 'firing shot' or one that will move the jack well back from its present position. Thus alerted, the other side can take steps to avert this danger either by placing a stopping shot (or 'block') in the firing line or by depositing one of their own bowls at the back.

I made one further unprofessional error when at the completion of each end I joined the other six players (the two skips were at the other end) in shuffling the bowls back towards the ditch. As the lead I should have gathered up the mat, put it in place and stood ready to deliver the jack just as soon as the skip had taken up his position as a length-marker. I was just wasting time by helping to collect the bowls, five pairs of feet can do this task perfectly adequately. I see that our local ladies use a very helpful rake-like device to manoeuvre their bowls to the rear of the rink. This seems to save much time and effort and is much more sophisticated than the shoe-shuffle that we men employ!

Also I suffered the humiliation of losing my bowls in the gathered mass of 16 – to the newish player all bowls look much the same. When I should have been ready on the mat, I was vainly trying to locate my bowls. Do get yourself organised, separate your bowls and put them together at one side and to the rear of the mat. This is especially important for the two leads. The game should flow, not be held up by unprofessional and avoidable interruptions.

After I had played two home matches it occurred to me that I should get some practice on slower greens than our Beach House Park tournament standard surfaces. I consequently put my name down for an away match, to be held one Saturday afternoon in September.

The weather forecast the night before was dreadful and in a panic I rang up my club captain to enquire whether friendly matches were played in the rain. I was told that they were, and advised to buy myself a set of waterproofs. Ever eager, I presented myself at a local sports shop early on the Saturday morning and purchased a proper set of white, waterproof (I hoped) over-trousers, high-necked jacket and hat. Apart from my bowls this was my greatest expense so far, but the honour of the club was at stake.

We had to meet at our club car park at 1.45 pm to start our five- or six-mile journey. After my early lunch it was still raining, still no phone call had come to tell me that the match had been called off. It was as well that I lingered for, at 1.15 pm, our match was cancelled.

On the subject of match play, do bear in mind that during an afternoon match there will probably be a break for tea, during which the two club captains or presidents will make a short speech. The home side welcome the visitors, wishing them a good game, and the visiting official responds. Do keep a respectful silence while the captains are on their feet and keep your seat until this time-honoured ceremony has been concluded and applauded. Only then should you make ready to resume the battle!

Two home matches won; one still to play. This last match was rather special, being our end of season club event, the president's team against the captain's. I was lead in the captain's four. All went well to begin with; I remembered to bring the jack and the two mats to the green and I bowled reasonably well, but then we all had to move up one in our playing positions.

This was a quite unexpected procedure and one adopted only for this particular friendly event. As the original lead, I now became number two and had to endeavour to keep the scorecard up to date. Later on we moved up again and I became number three and, as such, was responsible for signalling to the skip from the head. I had already had to bowl to a crowded head where rather more advanced shots were called for and I had little idea what information or advice to give the skip. In short, I was very much out of my depth. All the season I had rightly played as lead and had hardly tried the duties of the more senior members of the team. My weaknesses were now thrown into sharp relief.

Happily, this last match ended quite well, for at the following dinner and club prize-giving ceremony our four were each presented with a miniature bottle of whisky – for having lost so heavily and with such good grace! I shall always treasure that little bottle given to me amid a roomful of laughter and clapping club members. To be a good loser is as important as being a gracious winner.

As became glaringly apparent to me in that match, the various members of a bowls team have definite duties to perform. These should be clearly understood by those taking part in all games, other than singles, where you are one of a team and have well-defined parts to play in the team's success.

The fours game is the basic club and inter-club event. Here the team comprises: lead, second, third and skip. Each player uses only two bowls. In the triples game the team is made up of: lead, second and skip, each of whom uses three bowls. In the pairs game we have just the lead and skip, who are each allowed to use all four bowls.

I will use the fours team as an example, but the roles apply equally in the other combinations, although the second in the triples game will have to combine the duties of second and third player.

Before I start, a word to all members of a club team: having put your name down to play, check to see if you have been chosen, and if so, the time you have to appear, the dress required (greys or whites) and the venue of the match. This information will be posted on the club noticeboard. Initial or tick your name – if this is a club practice – to indicate that you have read the notice and will be available.

If you are unable to turn up or are likely to do a 'Godden' and be late, do let your club know as early as possible, so as not to let the whole team down. If you have been chosen as a reserve, you are still a member of the team and should make every effort to join them completely equipped to play if you are needed. Vital matches have been lost through the failure of a reserve to be available.

If you are to play an afternoon match do not stuff yourself with a heavy meal just before play – however, one author's advice to confine your lunch to a glass of water or fruit juice and an apple may be going a little too far! Remember that in a competitive match no player is permitted to have played on that rink that same day, except in the case of open tournaments (Law 12).

Your first duty is to report your presence, normally to your skip or club captain if he is in attendance. Pay any green fee or match money, ascertain which rink you have been allocated and ask if there is any equipment to be taken to the green. If you are playing in an away match you will obviously need to familiarise yourself with the facilities and make yourself comfortable before you are on the green. If you are playing at home, help any visitors to find their way about and in general act as a good host. The individual players' duties are as follows:

LEAD

It is the home lead's duty to have the two mats and the jack available on the rink. Before the game commences choose a convenient moment to have a word with the skip –

particularly if you have not previously played together – to ascertain his views on the positioning of the mat. Does he favour the mat back near the ditch or well forward? Is he content to leave this matter to your good judgement? Inform your skip of any weakness you have. Let him be forewarned so that he can take such points into account when planning his tactics. If you are unable to have a preliminary word with him – he may well have other matters on his mind – talk to the number three who can more easily contact the skip and report back to you.

Once the skip has made the introductions and shaken hands find time to have a friendly word with your opposite number. Enlarge the basic introduction and remember to use his first name. The rules state that the captain shall toss a coin to decide which team is to place the mat initially and bowl the first wood. Remember that in winning the toss one can either take the first bowl or, alternatively, nominate the other side to take premier position – it is a matter of tactics. Sometimes, particularly in Australia, the lead will conduct the toss, but under British rules (if not practice) it is the skip's duty.

Before a match commences there will be two trial ends, so that both sides can size up the rink and its characteristics. Each lead will cast the jack and deliver the first bowl for one of these two ends. For these trial ends most skips will favour a long jack, six feet back from the far ditch, but the mat need not be at the regulation starting distance.

You can change your bowls during this practice to see which type suits the conditions best. This is not permitted once the match has begun, and in important events the new bowls will need to be shown to the umpire to be checked for up-to-date stamping. They should also bear the correct stickers for that match.

No scores are taken during the trial end although the skip will signal the length and lie of your bowls. Note them well – the whole object of these two ends is to gauge the running of your bowls on your rink. You should assess the speed of the rink and the grass-line to be taken. Your future play will be based on your observations during these trials, so do not waste the time.

At the start of the match proper it is your job to place the mat in the prescribed manner. Glance at the skip at the opposite end of the rink – he may not agree that the mat is on a central line with the markers. When you prepare to cast the jack look to your skip, at whose feet you should target it, to check that he is ready and that you are quite sure of his wishes. You are placing the jack not to suit your own taste but to best serve the whole team. Remember in casting the jack you have to abide by the basic rules of delivery, with at least one foot entirely on or over the mat as the jack leaves your hand. Assuming that the jack comes to rest within the prescribed limits the skip will then endeavour to centre it.

You need to assist in this centring if centre lines are not marked on the rink and signal clearly the required correction. Many players signal the required correction by holding their hands or fingers the appropriate distance apart, but such close measures can be misinterpreted by the skip who is 25 yards away.

If you cast your jack less than two yards from the end ditch the skip will move it out to this minimum distance before centring it. Were you to over-shoot the jack into the ditch or over the side strings, or to cast it less than 25 yards from the front edge of the mat, it would be deemed 'improperly delivered' (Law 30) and the opposing lead would then cast the jack to his or his skip's preference. However, as the original lead you would still deliver your bowl first. The length of the cast jack cannot be challenged once both leads have each delivered one bowl; see Laws 29 and 30.

Now that the jack is in position, your basic duty is to deliver your two bowls so that they rest nearer to the jack than those of the opposing lead. You will not be successful at

Generally bowls behind (or just in front of) the jack are the best positioned. The bowl to the left of the jack can be displaced by an opposing bowl, being stopped by it – or can knock the side bowl away.

every attempt, but if you can gain a premier position six or seven times in every ten ends you will be earning your keep in the side.

To achieve this try not to deliver short woods that will distract following players or obstruct their bowls. Rather, you should bowl to a central resting line with your bowl either directly in front of or, preferably, behind the jack. This is more desirable than resting to the side of the jack where it will present a larger target for following players intent on moving your woods or the jack.

If by chance you do happen to bowl a short first wood on, say, your forehand so that it blocks further deliveries, do not switch to the other hand and then block that approach also. It is better to keep to the forehand and to try to move your first blocking bowl with one with more weight. Don't whatever you do leave two out in front. Most skips will prefer you to keep one hand, not switch about. Choose the best hand for one direction and stick to it, but if you wish use a backhand when you come back down the rink.

As I have previously stated, watch your bowl for the whole length of its run, assessing what corrections of line or length will be required, and acknowledge your skip's signals to that effect. Once your bowl has come to rest the possession of the rink passes to the other side. You should now be to the rear of the mat, well out of the line of sight of the next player. Similarly, that player should not have taken up his stance while you were in possession. You will now be well advised to watch the other lead's delivery and to note his grass-line and which hand he prefers.

Once your opposing lead's wood has come to rest you can regain your place on the mat with your second bowl. Look to the skip, who may well have instructions; perhaps a forehand delivery rather than a backhand. Any instructions (not suggestions!) will be signalled by a sweep of the hand curving in from the right- or left-hand side of the jack, or he may merely hold out his right or left arm. He may now quite possibly wish you to deliver a bowl 'round the back', behind the jack. If no instructions are forthcoming simply draw as close to the jack as you can. Resist the temptation to bowl a heavy wood and to try to knock off an opposing well-placed bowl – this is not the task of a number one unless he has been so instructed. As a general rule it is better to keep to your best hand, forehand or backhand (unless otherwise instructed), and not to worry about other woods which appear to be in the way of your normal delivery, unless you need to move these to make more room for following players to try their skills.

Your first two woods having been delivered, learn from any errors and seek to correct them as the game progresses. You can now retire to the top of the bank, the better to view the following deliveries and to keep the rink as clear as possible. Have a few friendly words with your opposite number but do not persist if he obviously wishes to concentrate on the game.

Once the number ones, twos and threes have delivered their woods, the six of you will walk up the rink to take your place behind the head or on the far bank. The skips will pass you as they cross over to make their deliveries. Hopefully, yours will have a word of praise for your efforts or at worse a word of encouragement for future ends!

Watch the skip's endeavours and how the fortunes of the game can change with each delivery. Be prepared to pick up the mat and place it should your side have won that end, but do not rush to do this before you are quite sure that the count has been completed and agreed by both number threes. However, as lead of the winning side you should not waste time helping to gather in the spent bowls – leave this to the other players.

Next, as this is not the first end, you can adjust the position of the mat to suit the preferences of your team as indicated by the skip. If your team is winning end after end do not experiment with different mat positions. They obviously have settled in and are having the best of the play, so retain that advantage. However, do use common sense and place the mat where you will ground the bowls on a well-grassed flat surface, avoiding bad or uneven patches.

If you lost the previous end, then obviously the other lead lays the mat and delivers the jack before making the first delivery. If this is the case it is a nice gesture to pick up the mat and jack and hand them to him. You might also locate and hand to him his first wood. It is not only courteous but helps to speed up the game.

SECOND OR NUMBER TWO

In this position you will need to have a pen or pencil for it is your responsibility to keep the score on a special scorecard which you must obtain beforehand and also on any scoreboard device on the bank. The provision of this board is the responsibility of the host team. The number threes will inform you of the count, you merely record it. Keep it up to date at all times, recording the number of ends played. You should consult with your opposite number so that at the end of the match your scorecards are in agreement and can be signed by the skips as the correct record. The date and the names of the various players should be correctly and legibly entered, and make sure that the completed and signed card is handed to the skip at the end of the game, not left in your pocket!

As to your bowling, the number two obviously follows the lead, alternating play with his opposite number. You should have been standing behind the leads observing their deliveries, gaining information on the speed of the green and on the grass-line and noting which bowls at the head belong to which team, who holds shot and if they are in front of the jack or behind it. You will no doubt have to rectify any faults or fill any gap.

It is again vital that the number two looks to his skip for he will be playing to instruction. He may simply be requested to draw to the jack if the lead has failed to bowl a scoring shot, or he may be needed to improve a good opening position, but very often he will be required to place his bowl in a given spot which may perhaps be devoid of any visual aiming point. This is a difficult task but you, as a budding number two, should have practised drawing to different points away from the jack; say two feet behind and to the right. The skip may well seek to help by holding a duster or the palm of his hand above the required position, but they seldom hold this temporary target in position long enough for it to be useful. They are forbidden by the Laws from placing any object on the green, although many a duster has been dropped!

The number two will often be asked to place one behind the jack to give his side potentially valuable back woods should the jack be knocked or trailed back from its original position. You may be asked to trail the jack yourself or to move front woods or scoring woods already in position. You might be required to play a running shot to open up the head for the number three or skip, without leaving your bowls short to obstruct them. You could even be instructed to produce a drive or firing shot, although this will be a rare occurrence. Never ever drive unless told to by the skip.

A good number two must, therefore, be versatile and able to play all types of shot with confidence. He is certainly not there just to make up the numbers. He should be a well practised, experienced player. I make this point because it used to be the fashion to introduce new players into the second position. Some clubs apparently still keep to this system but it is now usual to start as lead and graduate through the team in numerical order.

There is, however, much to be said for specialising in a given position if you excel there or enjoy it. A specialist lead or number two is an invaluable asset to any team. But a number two should remember his position. He is not number three and should not signal to the skip. The last thing the skip requires is two conflicting sources of information.

NUMBER THREE

This player will normally be a very experienced bowler who has played in matches over several years and graduated to his present position as deputy to the skip. He should have a good knowledge of the Laws of the game.

He will know well that he must be equipped with chalk to mark his skip's touchers and a special bowler's measure. The third's duty to agree the score at the termination of each end often necessitates using the measure to check the distances between the bowl and the jack. Having agreed the number and ownership of the scoring bowls, he passes this information on to the number twos so that they can enter it on their scorecards and bring the scoreboard up to date. The deputy will also signal the information up to his skip at the other end of the rink.

The number three should be very observant over the count. He can very easily miss shots that should have been included in the tally. His opposite number is there to represent his own team's interests not to correct the score of the other side. Do not hesitate to query a shot. Do not give away hard-earned points. Remove only bowls you have conceded.

Although the number three may join the skip at the jack end of the rink to observe the lie of the leads' and the number twos' bowls and to discuss tactics with the skip before returning to the mat end to deliver his two bowls, it is more usual for him to remain with the team behind the mat. There he acts as the skip's deputy, keeping an eye on all his players, watching points and generally supervising proceedings.

Above. *Surveying an open head. Note the number two's scorecard.*

Below. *A scoring exercise. The bowl on the jack scores one but the bowls with the bird logo stop further points being added. Had the shot bowl not been there the opposition would score two.*

He can offer encouragement and even advice to the new, nervous or off-form player. This should be done while the bowler is off the mat – he should not act as coach and make corrections while the player is about to make his delivery! Nevertheless, I have often been taken to one side or on to the top of the bank by a good, observant number three and given valuable advice that has helped future deliveries. A good understanding third has earned his place in the side before he has delivered a single wood.

The experienced player will no doubt have a good idea of what the skip requires of him as each head is built up, but he must on all occasions look to the skip before each delivery. Which hand does he suggest? A short blocking shot or a drive? More likely he will be asked for a heavyish shot to open up the head or a bowl well behind the jack to pair an opposing back wood. The skip may well ask you to wrest out a troublesome bowl, one that is making a possible count of five into a mere one. Move it and you have scored a potential four extra shots – five if your wood stops and does not run on. You may be required only to make a standard draw to the jack. Such a well-placed wood may save five or six points if it ends nearer the jack than those of the opponent; a 'second wood' can be nearly as helpful, reducing the other's score to just one.

You should be able to deliver accurately any shot in the book. You must have every faith in your captain and accept his instructions without question. Support him to the hilt, not letting other members of the team question the skip's tactics or play.

Once the threes have delivered their last woods it is time to change positions with the skips. Before leaving the mat end, however, it is usual to place the leading skip's bowl just in front of the mat ready for him to pick up – perhaps giving it a rub over should it be wet or dirty. As you cross on the rink, the skip will probably have a few words with you to explain the position and his basic aim. Keep such discussion, and indeed all such information, very much low-key. Do not let the other skip in on your tactics.

Once the number three is at the head with the other players he ensures that they are all behind the action, ideally behind the most rearward of the bowls. I prefer to stand out of the way on the bank where I can gain a better view of play, but the number three will be on the rink ready to signal to the skip or mark his touchers. It is important that the six players do not move around or otherwise distract the skips who are about to bowl. It is number three's responsibility as the senior player present to see that the players abide by these rules.

The skip has just left the head and should not require any signalled information until the position of the bowls in the head has been changed. He may, however, require you to pin-point a hidden jack. At this point he will need to know how short or long his delivery was so that he can make any corrections and also if the count has been changed. The experienced number three will know how to signal silently the number of shots up or down by holding the appropriate number of fingers upright or groundwards. He will also be able to signal the required distance by holding his hand that distance from the ground. All such signals should be quite clear, and the distances should not be exaggerated, otherwise the skip may inadvertently over-correct in his next delivery. The number three must signal only when the skip has possession of the rink and not when the other player is on the mat. If you are a number three and are not sure, don't guess. It is better to call the skip up to the head than to feed incorrect information. Just place your hand up on top of your own head and he should understand that he is being invited to see for himself. One further point: you should be ready to mark with chalk any touchers your skip may deliver and to remove any dead woods from the ditch.

Before beginning the count the number three must make quite sure that both skips have bowled both their woods and that the end is consequently over. He should see that nobody moves bowls that are possibly in the count before the scores have been agreed or before any measuring has been completed.

Lastly, after the measuring and agreement of the score, the number three ensures that the bowls are being moved back and that the winning lead is laying the mat and is ready to commence the next end with the minimum of delay.

SKIP

The Laws of the game state simply: 'The skip shall have sole charge of his team and his instructions shall be observed by his players. With the opposing skip he shall decide all disputed points and when both agree their decision shall be final . . .'

Beyond this premise he has, of course, many other duties or functions to perform. The skip should have introduced his team to the other players and checked that all necessary equipment is available and that all players are on parade and wearing the correct shoes. The two skips will then toss a coin to decide which side will bowl first in the initial end. They then take up positions at the far end of the rink and direct play from there until it is their turn to bowl.

The skip of the winning side should direct his lead as to the position to which the jack should be cast. This is done by standing at that spot – or better still slightly to one side of the centre rink-marker – that is unless he has earlier given clear verbal instructions. He will then need to centre the jack, provided that it has been delivered within the prescribed area, and glance up the rink to check that the mat is central and straight.

The preferred manner of indicating the required length for the cast jack without obstructing the lead's view of the rink marker.

The skip must indicate by hand signals how far in front of the jack each newly-delivered bowl has finished, or the distance it has travelled past the target. The side distance can be judged by the bowler; the fore and aft distances cannot and must be indicated so that corrections of pace can be made. For this reason do not exaggerate the signal – if the signal is four feet instead of the correct two, the best of players will still be two feet out through no fault of their own if they have corrected to the skip's directions.

The skip must have chalk handy to mark any touchers. This chalk cross or tick is not normally added until the next bowl has left the bowler's hand and is progressing up the rink, so that the movement does not distract the concentration of that bowler. However, the Laws imply that the toucher should be marked before the next player takes his stance on the mat. This arises from Law 50 which relates to 'possession of the rink', which passes from one player to the next 'as soon as each bowl shall have come to rest, . . . time being allowed for marking a toucher'. It is safer to mark touchers before the next bowl is delivered, but this is seldom done to save interrupting the flow of the game. If skip, number three or marker have to chalk touchers it would be best to inform the other players of your intended method or timing of the action so that there is no misunderstanding. In time perhaps a more advanced method of marking touchers can be introduced that will be simpler than chalking, which can disturb the bowl. Some bowlers are even advocating doing away with touchers altogether, but for the time being the Laws state that they shall be marked with chalk.

The skip should remove from the ditch any dead bowls or woods that have strayed out of the rink. He should keep an eye open for bowls delivered with the wrong bias which will consequently progress towards the adjacent rink and intercept them before they do any damage. The skip should confine the marking of touchers and the removal of dead bowls to those of his own side.

He should naturally – as a bowler – be friendly to his opposite number and indulge in a little humorous banter as the opportunity arises. He will, of course, applaud a good shot from the opposition as he would one from his own players. The skips must always consult on any matter that may crop up affecting the play, the rules or their interpretation. If you think a member of his team is at fault mention it to his skip and not to the player.

Players should not be afraid to ask their skip to point out the position of the jack if this happens to be hidden from view by bowls resting in front of the target. The skip will normally do this by placing his hand (perhaps holding a white duster) above the jack, keeping it in place long enough for it to serve its purpose. Such indication must be removed before the player is ready to bowl.

Apart from these simple points concerning the conduct of play, very much more is expected of a skip. Most games are won or lost by the skip; not so much by his bowling skill as by the way he controls and encourages the rest of his team and his mastery (or otherwise) of tactics.

It may well be that no existing experienced skip with years of service behind him will read this book, angled as it is at the new bowler, but the novices who aspire to leadership may care to bear in mind some of my views on the attributes that make the succesful team captain.

He should be enthusiastic and encouraging to all his players. A little clap for a good bowl lifts the player, as does a smile and a few words as the players pass him on their way up the rink.

I like a skip to be positive; to lead by giving clear instructions that leave the player in no doubt as to what he is being asked to do. Decisive thinking and very clear signals are required. At the same time, the skip should keep half an eye on the player. Only this week I saw an excellent skip bending down over the head to indicate the suggested line of approach and which opposing bowls to take out. However, his signals were entirely wasted because the bowler had his back to the skip as he was picking up his next wood! It was not entirely the skip's fault, but he should remember to see if he is commanding attention before giving instructions.

I find it difficult to hear a skip's verbal instructions from the far end of the rink, especially in windy conditions, so it is useful to the players if a skip speaks up, faces the players, and projects his voice. At Worthing we have a wonderful Sergeant-Major type skip whose instructions can surely be heard all over the town!

Skips should appreciate that the rest of the team like to know the state of game: which side is holding shot and by how many. This is not at all clear from the mat.

I like a forgiving skip! One who will say 'bad luck' or 'next time' when one bowls a loose wood – as we all do from time to time. It is unhelpful in the extreme to be told the obvious; 'you're wide', or 'too short'. The poor player needs encouragement to bowl a snorter next time. The skip should be a good diplomat, calming rather than ruffling. The captain should be of a calm temperament, not given to panic when his side is five or six down on one end or lying 15 or so down in the match. That is when clear thought is needed and where tactics come in if your side is being out-played. That is the time to really know your team, to motivate them, not to be seen to lose interest in the game. I, in my short bowling life, have seen some truly remarkable recoveries from seemingly impossible positions. This recovery should stem from the enthusiasm of the skip.

Many skips could, I feel, be more communicative, Most discuss play with their number three, but all too few trouble to bring the other members of the team into the discussion or even to give a brief pep-talk before the game starts. The lead will usually have to ask about the position of the mat when he could have been told about the skip's preferences before the game began. I would like the skip occasionally to come up to the mat and rally his team while the number three takes his place at the head from where he can better see the position before his turn comes to bowl. Such a ploy may take a little time but it would show that the captain is a caring one and also an individualist. Above all be amenable and approachable.

The parson's cat should also be an observant cat! He should watch over not only his own team and the way they are bowling but also observe the other team and assess their strong points and, more importantly, their weaknesses. If they all favour the forehand shot he should try to block that approach, forcing them to play backhand shots. If they favour long jacks, he will obviously see that his lead bowls short jacks. If they favour trailing the jack, he will signal his number two or three to deliver the woods well back behind the jack. Watch the opposition as much as your own players.

Apart from these desirable attributes, the skip will undoubtedly have been chosen because of his experience and capabilities as a club bowler. He will have command of all types of shot, and will know when to play them, as well as his knowledge of tactics and his thorough understanding of the governing Laws. He is a rare bird and should be treated with due respect.

THE DUTIES OF A MARKER

You may be asked to act as a marker for two club members who are playing a singles game, so it is useful to know the basic dos and don'ts of such an important duty. You will need a piece of chalk, a measure, a scorecard and an understanding of the Laws of Lawn Bowls.

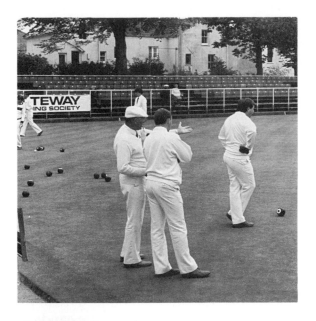

Left. *As skip, take time to think the problem out, decide where the wood will do the most good, communicate your tactics and offer encouragement.*

Below. *An experienced marker standing well back and to one side of the rink, clearly concentrating on the game and well prepared to carry out her duties.*

A marker is needed when two persons are playing a singles match of some consequence, perhaps in a competition or tournament. It is the marker whom you see on television standing behind the head and signalling (with lollipop-type sticks) his idea of the shots held by one or other player. These 'lollipops' are only used in televised games – they are not mentioned in the Laws – and in normal play the marker will indicate the number of shots held only when asked to do so. Although the marker is not an umpire or a coach – the role is quite restricted – his duties are important and should be taken seriously.

In essence he enables the game to proceed without the need for the two players to be continually walking up to inspect the head or perform other duties. He acts as their eyes but in a strictly neutral manner. First he ensures that, after being centred, the jack has travelled the minimum 25 yards from the front of the mat. If it has overrun the maximum length he moves it back to the regulation six feet from the ditch. He should return a jack that has been delivered into the ditch, and should also check from the head end that the mat has been correctly laid in a central position.

Having centred the jack, the marker should retire behind it and stand to one side, completely still, and in general ensure that he does not distract the players. He should not obstruct the rink-boundary markers.

He should mark with chalk any touchers and clear the ditch or rink of any dead bowls. On the clearance of dead woods the Laws state that this shall be 'with the agreement of both opponents' and he should seek the players' agreement to this duty before the game commences, although in my experience this is taken for granted. He could also ask when the players favour the marking of touchers: before the next bowl is delivered or while it progresses down the rink.

My first marker correctly introduced himself to both players, asked which was the challenger (normally the first-named of the two players) and announced that the challenger's score would be given first. He then stated, for our agreement, the handicap starting score. Next he sought our agreement to his marking the touchers before the next bowl was delivered and our permission to remove dead bowls at his sole discretion.

The marker will be required to pinpoint with a bank-marker the position of a jack sent into the ditch during play and, if asked to do so by a player, he may likewise indicate the position of any toucher that may also rest in the ditch. He must when asked, and only then, give the required information to the player in possession of the rink. His answers must be brief and to the point, stating how far short or long the bowl has rested. He should not then give a résumé of the relative position of other woods and most certainly not make any suggestion of the best method of play, such as 'try the backhand'!

If either player tries it on and seeks too much information or advice, then the marker should invite him to made his own inspection. The player may correctly ask if he is holding shot, and if so by how many, in which case the answer is simply 'Yes' or 'No' and the score. The marker must give this information from a visual inspection only – no measuring can be undertaken until the end is completed. This is only an unofficial understanding of the position at that time and in no way effects the final score, which the players – not the marker – mutually agree.

Having moved forward to inspect the head and answered any question or marked a toucher, the marker immediately retires to the side before the player settles to make his delivery. After the end has been completed, his marking duties come into play. Once the players have agreed the score the marker completes that entry on the scorecard, and calls the total over to the players for their agreement. He also brings up to date any scoreboard that is in use and amends the number of ends played. At the completion of the game he gets both players to agree and sign the scorecard before handing it in to the authority controlling the competition or tournament.

If the players cannot agree the score or if so requested by them, the marker will be required to bring the measure into play and to determine which bowl is the nearer to the jack. As I have previously stated, the act of measuring can only be carried out when the end has been completed. In measuring every effort must be taken not to move the jack or the bowls that are in contention. A special wedge (or a coin) can be used to stop the last bowl of the end from toppling over into a new lie, once the permitted 30 seconds settling time has elapsed (Law 53).

For your measuring exercise it is best to rest the feeler of the measure just short of the jack – say $^1/_{16}$ th of an inch from the point on the circumference of the jack nearest the bowl to be first measured. Hold this firmly in place on the ground and stretch the measure out in a straight line to the *nearest* point on the bowl so that it just touches. The measure should be capable of being fixed at that or any required distance. Now repeat the exercise to the next bowl in contention, remembering to leave the end of the measure the same small distance from the jack. If on this first measure you find that the second wood is the nearest, go back to re-measure the first – just in case the set position of the measure has moved. If there is still more than about a quarter of an inch difference between the two woods you can clearly declare the nearer one to be the shot. If the distance is smaller you may need to re-measure with the tip of the instrument right up to the jack, but this is not normally necessary and by leaving the initial gap you have made sure that you have not moved the jack. You should clearly indicate the shot wood but do not move this or any other bowls – you may be asked to re-measure. Only the player (or in the case of a dispute, the umpire) should do this, since there may be other woods to be measured for a possible second, third or even fourth shot. Remember 'all measurements shall be made to the nearest point of each object'. The feeler on the special bowler's measure should be placed to the jack, not to the bowl.

In most cases the distances are clearly in favour of one wood and the players agree without resort to the measure – which takes up valuable time – but a player should not be afraid to call for its use. It is up to the person claiming the shot to confirm his views via the measure, if he requests so to do.

It must be stated that unless you have some considerable experience of playing in singles games and have played bowls for a few seasons you should not offer yourself as a marker. You may not, for example, know the meaning of a player's silent signals to you for information or yet be able correctly to read the position and thus give – albeit in good faith – incorrect information. If you wish to become a good marker and so have the opportunity not only of helping fellow bowlers but also of watching good players, do study experienced markers at work and study section 72 of the Laws of the game.

As a novice player you will hardly be called upon to act as an umpire, for such a person should have undergone special training and been officially appointed, but the basic outlines of his duties are also given in the Laws, under section 73.

Tuition—Bowling Courses

I endeavoured to receive some tuition before first venturing on to a green only to be told that the coaching courses held locally were for experienced players 'of one year's or more playing experience' and not for novices. In theory at least, according to the English Bowling Association coaching system, each club should have its own qualified instructor or a coach able and willing to give sound advice to the new member. However, this is not always the case and many would–be bowlers no doubt wish to learn about the game before they join a club.

ADVANCED BOWLS COACHING HOLIDAY, WORTHING

The courses run by Roy Downing – Britain's first professional bowls coach – are held in Worthing during 18 weekly periods from late April–early May to the beginning of October, with a break in August while national or international tournaments are in progress on the Beach House greens. Details of the courses are available from Roy Downing, and his and other instructional courses are advertised in the magazines *Bowls International* and *World Bowls.* You will need to book early.

Feeling in need of further tuition, I joined one of the courses which took place in September 1985. The courses are advertised as advanced bowls coaching holidays under the personal supervision of Roy Downing.

Roy joined the first coaching courses held by the English Bowling Association at Crystal Palace in 1973. This select group of five (under Tommy Taylor) were pioneers as far as British coaching was concerned and they drew up the first syllabus for the teaching of the game in this country. These five were subsequently appointed as regional coaches and later themselves appointed and trained county coaches.

Roy Downing was well fitted to act as a regional EBA-qualified coach for, apart from his bowling skill and experience, he was formerly a professional footballer, a top sprinter and a boxer, as well as a qualified PE teacher. In 1977 he decided to coach bowls on a professional basis, charging for his expert tuition (as a consequence he was banned under the rules then from playing in competitive bowling events). He began his courses at Worthing as weekend events, commencing weekly courses in 1980. In addition he has coached in Spain, Florida and Australia, and has recently been employed to promote bowls in Ibiza and Tenerife and to organise bowling holidays in Australia and New Zealand. In January 1986 he opened the Worthing Bowls and Equipment Centre in

50

Brighton Road, Worthing, a few hundred yards from the Beach House Park greens. The shop has a helpful bowls testing rink downstairs – I believe this to be the first such facility in the British Isles – where one can try out various sizes and types of bowl before making a purchase. The correct choice of bowl is so vital to one's future progress and enjoyment that one wonders why such small practice areas have not been introduced previously. It is one of many ideas Roy has brought back from his travels, in this case from Australia. I have learned recently that at least one other British supplier has followed his example.

Each week's course, which is limited to 12 people, begins at 10.00 am on the Monday. We were ushered into the convenient and comfortable Bowl Inn restaurant adjacent to the greens and seated around a table. Introductions were made while coffee was being served. Next we each were asked to select a coloured disc. In this way we were divided into four different teams. This selection was not quite a random one as Roy amended it slightly so that husbands and wives were not in the same team. He had obviously learned from past experience!

We now had four teams of three, each with a distinguishing colour, and corresponding stickers for our bowls. Playing positions were chosen: lead, second and skip. After being briefed on the running of the week's programme we began our first session on the green.

The students gathered at Worthing from many parts of the country were a mixed group – six ladies and six men. These included two married couples and one brother and sister. Ages ranged probably from 30 to over 60. With three exceptions, myself and a newly-retired married couple, all were quite experienced club players. In one case, I understand, fellow club members had combined to pay the week's expenses and I assume that the benefits of the coaching were subsequently to be passed on to them.

As we gathered on the green that hot sunny Monday in September it was soon apparent why Roy did not take beginners. He had no intention of teaching us the basics, his advertised task being to correct our technique and improve our game. Consequently he first coupled the teams – and told us to play our natural game. He obviously needed to identify our strong points and weaknesses, so that as the week progressed he could work on these and show us where improvements could be made. Much to my surprise, he started to record our first session on a video camera. This was later to be played back to us, much to our embarrassment!

In the afternoon we were 'individually assessed'. The faults shown up by the morning's game were explained and suggestions made to enable us to rectify them. The most common errors arose from our delivery – our lack of balance and flow. We tended to push the bowl and to bring the right hand around away from our shoulder line. Some of us over-did the step forward with the left foot. Most failed to stand correctly on the mat so that the line of delivery was often narrow and the bowl ended well off-centre.

The second morning was billed as 'individual coaching, correction of faults'. For most of the morning we played normal games as Roy came around among us giving advice, endeavouring to correct our stance and the all-important delivery. From time to time we were called together for general discussion on various aspects of the game. Questions were, of course, asked and answered.

In the afternoon we played the first round of a triples competition. However, our chosen playing positions were moved forward one position. That is, the lead (myself) acted as number two who took over as skip who, in turn, tried his skill as lead. The triples team competition was a very serious affair, played under the correct rules with no short cuts. Scorecards were kept and handed in. A great improvement was evident and we were playing as teams.

Wednesday morning was an exciting one, given over to the demonstration of various

Above. *Two faults. My follow-through has not been straight, making the delivery narrower than intended. Also the mat is not centred on the rink-marker.*

Below. *Roy Downing discussing faults and tactics with his students.*

Left. *Norman King always concentrates on the correct grip, reversing the bowl and adjusting his fingers' position before he turns his wrist to deliver.*

Above. *Having stepped forward on to the mat, his eyes are well up on his point of aim, and he is about to take his left hand away and commence the backward swing.*

shots and our subsequent practice of these. The demonstration period was enhanced by the fact that Norman King joined Roy to demonstrate his method of holding the bowl and his upright but so smooth delivery. We were told how to increase the length of delivery by increasing the back-swing and/or the forward step as the delivery is made. In the subsequent practice session Norman King and Roy Downing took us through various exercises in length control. We had to bowl to various markers, so short, medium and long shots were called for, with points awarded for especially good deliveries. At this time we were concerned only with judging and bowling to different length targets. At other times we were concerned with line – taking the correct 'green'. The difficulty is to combine an accurate length with a perfect line. Practice makes perfect, or at least shows up the difficulties which have to be surmounted. The morning's practice was hard work but certainly rewarding.

In the afternoon we started with an all-too-brief discussion on tactics: moving the position of the mat if deemed necessary after the first end so as to put off an on-form opponent; changing the length of the jack, and so forth. We also discussed some of the problems presented to the captain in building up a good head, and the instructions to be given to number two in an effort to turn a bad position into a winning one. Pinpoint positioning is one thing, but where will your bowl do the most good?

At the end of a very enjoyable day we had another triples game, again with our coach keeping a weather eye open. He seemed to have eyes in the back of his head, giving advice and correcting those troublesome faults which were so deeply ingrained in us.

Thursday was a relatively restful day, with the morning devoted to another round of our triples competition. We again changed the playing position by all moving up one, so that by Friday each bowler would have played in a different position and each team would have played against the other three.

Thursday afternoon was left free on the programme. This would have enabled Roy to accommodate the full course should any other session have been rained off. However, we had been blessed with wonderful dry and sunny weather all through the week.

We now come to Friday when, as usual, we were all on parade embarrassingly early. It was the last round of our triples competition and we were to play in our original positions in this session. We were told how the various teams stood in regard to the running total of points scored. We, the yellow team, were lying third some 12 points behind the leader. Now at last we could put into practice all the advice we had been given over the past few days. Although our more serious faults should have been ironed out by this time, we had all of course enjoyed the same tuition! There were remarkably few stray bowls. We were too intent on our game to watch the scores on the adjoining rink and I was delighted when my three bowls on the last end finished in a perfect close line just behind the jack. I ended the week with three perfect shot bowls. Our team scored five or six on that end and had a very healthy overall score.

I could not resist pointing out my three near-perfect bowls to Roy who was watching the other rink. With a smile he said that, depending on the last bowl now progressing down the rink, my yellow team would come up from third place to take the trophy. That last bowl on the other rink was good but not good enough to change the scores. As the yellow lead with three scoring bowls, I felt more elated than any World Champion! I and the rest of the yellow team will always treasure our Worthing trophies. Aside from this award we all very much enjoyed our week's bowling course.

You, however, will rightly require to know if it was beneficial. As far as I am concerned the answer is a most emphatic 'yes'. Roy could not in a week make a champion of me – a novice in my first year of play – but I may give him another opportunity! Certainly at the end of the week I felt more confident and, therefore, more at ease on a rink with experienced players. I now knew how some things should be done, such as casting a jack accurately and making correcting signals in a clear, proficient manner. I now stepped on to the mat with a confident air and had a reasonable delivery knowing my duty as a team member and as lead.

I was a better all-round bowler and would in future give less offence on the green and be better placed to uphold the excellent reputation of the game and of my own club. I was indebted to Roy for a most enjoyable and instructive week. I will undoubtedly go back for more and seek out similar coaching courses in other bowling centres.

BEGINNERS' COURSE AT BOURNEMOUTH

I noticed an advertisement for this course in *Bowls International* magazine in January 1986. The text read: 'Put yourself in the hands of a true professional, the popular National Advanced Coach, Bill Shipton. You'll get expert personalised tuition – not gimmicks – with no more than 12 people . . . outdoor instruction on Meyrick Park's first-class greens . . .'.

Some seven months after delivering my first bowls I no longer considered myself a beginner! Obviously, I should have attended this a year earlier, before joining the Worthing Club, but I had not then been aware that such coaching was available. Still better late than never, as they say. However, my wife Jean was very much a novice, so much so that we were given to understand that she would not be considered for membership of our local Ladies Club until she had acquired basic skills and experience – seemingly a vicious circle! We were later to discover that our information had been incorrect in this regard, and I am happy to report that Jean and her friend have well and truly been welcomed into their new club. Various experienced members have been delegated to play with them and have given valuable advice and inspiration.

As I had by this time begun writing this book it seemed a good idea for us to take part in this two-day Bournemouth course, which would help Jean and on which I could report for the benefit of other would-be bowlers.

We joined the course in April 1986 with two friends, another Geoff and Jean. Our friends were golfers with next to no knowledge of bowling, so our party therefore comprised three non-bowlers plus myself with less than 12 months' experience.

On the Thursday morning when the course started we were picked up from our hotel just before 9.30 am by the holiday company's mini-bus and driven to the upper greens at Meyrick Park. We arrived at this beautiful and secluded setting well before the advertised starting time of 10.00 am and were greeted by Bill Shipton. He fitted out those who needed them with bowls and light-weight flat-soled shoes, rightly not permitting some of the not-quite-flat sports shoes that some students were wearing. We were soon all fully equipped as we were using only two and not four bowls.

The course comprised eleven people ranging in age from perhaps 40 to 55. I was certainly the odd-man-out having had some experience – eight or nine of the others were true novices, although they had at least watched the game on television or played a few friendly roll-ups.

There were none of the late R.T. Harrison's pre-green lectures or films, but on a two-day course we might well have felt cheated if we had not been on the green every moment of that short time. This lack of preliminary lectures is not to say that we did not have mini-lectures, demonstrations and discussions. These were nicely interposed with practice and this I think is the correct approach.

Bill Shipton is a highly qualified coach who has run professional courses since 1981. He is an English Bowls Council coach, the Dorset County Coach since 1973, a National Advanced Coach and an umpire. Indeed, this year he is the Chairman of the English Bowls Umpires Association. In putting over his points he uses an agreeable, friendly and humorous style. There was no undue rush to keep to a predetermined timetable, for questions were invited and dealt with at length.

Obviously in the first session Bill had to confine himself to basics – the bowls, the question of bias, the various grips, placing the mat and the stance on the mat. We then had our first practice deliveries. As will always happen, these initial bowls were all over the place and mostly very short of length. This enabled Bill to go around giving personal advice to the players. He checked the grip, tried to get rid of the wobbles, corrected the angle of the feet and body as the student stood on the mat and endeavoured to get more swing and less throw into the deliveries.

In some cases he took the player off to another vacant rink to give his personal attention to the troublesome points. This avoided disturbing the play and practice the others were enjoying on the two rinks we were using that morning.

Initially, Bill was rightly concerned with our line – our ability to deliver a bowl so that it would return to the central line. We were not yet concerned with length, indeed, to my surprise we rarely used a jack in our exercises. At one time we practised delivering down a line by bowling over a small, positioned mat. This exercise concentrates the mind on 'choosing and using' a line.

The question of bias was well put over with the use of a blackboard and with Bill's 'magic' magnetised board on which he placed targets and curved lines representing typical delivery lines. Even those who were quite sure that the length of a delivery must

Right. *Practising accuracy in delivery, between two mats placed on the rink.*

Below. *Even more accuracy is required here in bowling over one small mat, representing the point of the arc as the bowl starts to curve into the jack.*

Not relaxed enough! The right hand on the ground shows a lack of balance and the forward step is a little long.

affect the required line of delivery were convinced that this was not the case once Bill had completed his demonstration.

Bill emphasised the importance of delivering the jack correctly and to a predetermined length. He gave very good advice on future practice – for example, not to bowl to pre-placed centrally positioned jacks but to leave a cast jack where it rested and then bowling to this off-centre target. He advocated having another person with you at practice. This makes it less tiring and also provides competition – a most important factor in one's play and progress.

The first day's two sessions were quickly over but much had been accomplished and our groundwork was well established. At this point Bill gave us our own copy of the Laws of the game, as formulated by the International Bowling Board. The eighth edition of the Laws was published in 1986 and has been reproduced here in Appendix I.

However well conducted a day's tuition, cannot alas turn you into a seasoned bowler and on the second day the same basic faults were still in evidence. Some had not learned to check the bowls for the correct bias side before their delivery. Many were still bowling narrow, mainly because they were placing their front foot directly down the rink and not at the grass-line. Bowls were being bumped – delivered from well above the green as the bowler was not low enough to the ground. Bowls were being pushed. In general the new players were too rushed – anxious to get on the mat and to get rid of their bowl – aiming at, rather than to, the jack. All these very common errors were explained

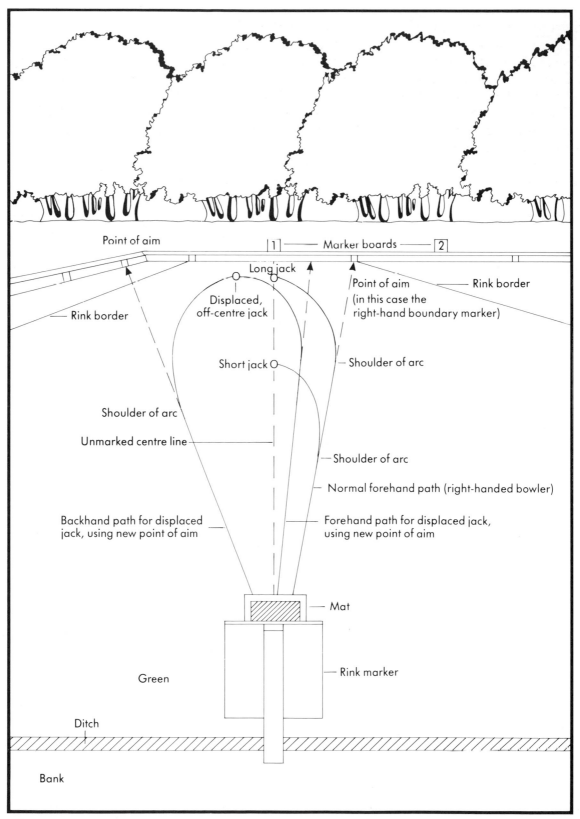

Point of aim

Marker boards

1 | 2

Long jack

Point of aim
(in this case the
right-hand boundary marker)

Rink border

Displaced,
off-centre jack

Rink border

Shoulder of arc

Short jack

Shoulder of arc

Shoulder of arc

Unmarked centre line

Shoulder of arc

Normal forehand path (right-handed bowler)

Backhand path for displaced
jack, using new point of aim

Forehand path for displaced jack,
using new point of aim

Mat

Green

Rink marker

Ditch

Bank

Different positioned jacks. Adjust the length rather than the line to reach the long or short jack. For the displaced jack aim wider and use more weight to reach it on the back hand as it is further away and the grass is unworn.

by Bill who again took those who were having special difficulty off to another rink where corrections could be made on a personal level.

As the morning drew to a close Bill Shipton gathered us around him to tell us in general terms of bowls etiquette and of the friendliness of bowlers. He wished us good luck and informed us that we all now possessed the basic skills and knowledge of the game; and that we should now join a local club and perfect our technique there.

The course closed at this point at lunchtime on the second day although our hotel reservations took us on to the following morning. We consequently had a spare afternoon and evening. Two groups of four from the course took advantage of this to book rinks for the afternoon so that we could test our skills. This was an interesting exercise for our party – we decided to play a standard doubles game.

Initially the ladies played as number ones while we acted as skips. The ladies, having delivered the jack, tended to step off the mat to gather their first bowl without stopping to signal the correct centring of the target – too much eagerness to get on with the game! Obviously, after only three half-days' tuition, the heads tended to be rather large and well spaced and the many short woods would later block the following deliveries. All skips will know this difficulty.

We were now playing with full sets of four bowls so that two of our party needed to hire sets from the green-keeper. One lady now experienced great difficulty in gripping hers and they were sliding prematurely from her hand during delivery. The reason was simply that the bowls were two or three sizes too large. Bill had on the first morning stressed the importance of having the correct size of bowl. He suggested that before buying a second-hand set from perhaps a fellow club member one should ask to try them for a few days. I treated these over-large bowls with 'Grippo'. This helped slightly, but the basic problem meant justice could not be done to Jean's prowess.

Still, we had an enjoyable couple of games. In the second one we changed positions so that the ladies acted as skips. In this new and unusual situation, they failed to signal back to us the length our bowls lay from the jack but this was one of the aspects of play that had not been covered in the beginners' course. One cannot, however, fault Bill's coverage of the essentials.

I think we shall be back again next year for a progressive course or even to try to manage a few days' bowling holiday on these delightfully situated greens. In that way we could perhaps take advantage of brief personal coaching, for I noticed that while we were playing the friendly game on the Friday afternoon Bill was coaching a husband and wife on another rink. I enquired about the cost of the bowling element in our package holiday and was told that it was £18.00 (inclusive of £5.70 per person in green fees). This represented very good value and my only reservation about the course was that it was so short. I put this complaint to Bill who explained that the course was primarily designed to get the beginners started on a firm and sound foundation after which they needed to think for themselves, putting their newly gained knowledge into practice.

A final word on coaching. It could well be that your local club or even your local authority run courses or training sessions for beginners or would-be bowlers. Bill informs me that he, as Dorset County Coach, has trained some 40 club instructors and five other coaches within the National Coaching Scheme.

By now every English club should have had available a coaching manual. Under the English Bowls Coaching Scheme some 2,500 instructors have received their certificates. Likewise 450 coaches and 21 advanced coaches have been trained. Also various coaching workshops have been established. These trained personnel are available to help you; seek them out. Your club secretary should be able to help.

Indoor Bowls

As the all-too-short British outdoor bowling season drew to a close at the end of September, so talk tended to swing round to the indoor bowling season. Seemingly, most of the members of my outdoor club already belonged to one of the two local indoor clubs, both of which were private, as opposed to municipal, concerns.

I was strongly advised to put my name down for the larger of the two – Worthing Indoor Bowls Club – as there was a very long waiting list. It has only one indoor 'green' and play is therefore restricted to five, or at the most six, rinks; on popular days and at peak times there must be quite a scramble for games. The need to restrict the number of members is also self-evident, indeed most senior members must feel that half of the present membership of 525 would be more sensible. The management committee has, however, to balance its books and an Indoor Bowling Club is an expensive luxury, even when many of the duties are undertaken by members acting in an honorary capacity. Also it is restricted to the winter season – October to April – but this is not the case with all indoor bowling clubs.

Having filled in my application form and been proposed and seconded by existing full members of the club, I was in due course notified that my application had been accepted by the committee. Accepted, that is, as an associate member – I would have to wait my turn to become a full member. I am told that this progression might take two years or more, so popular is bowls becoming and so long is the waiting list.

The treasurer was not prepared to wait that long for my dues and I was very promptly invited to pay my entrance fee of £40.00. Half was payable immediately (the balance on becoming a full member) along with the annual subscription which in November 1985 came to £16.50.

It is not only fair, but necessary to explain this cost. In addition to its bowling facilities, this comfortable modern club contains a good bar, a restaurant, a lounge/television room, and rooms for snooker and cards. Also, while still only an associate member, there were various opportunities for me to join the full members for games of bowls. All in all, considering that the club is open from 9.30 am until 10.00 pm seven days a week, the subscription is surely very good value for money.

The details I have quoted relate of course to my club, but they would not differ materially from those of other clubs in other districts.

I must, however, record my impression that a privately-run indoor bowling club such as this is not the best place to begin one's bowling career. Its function is to provide facilities for experienced players rather than tuition or practice for novices. Indeed, one of the rules of this club is that proposed members should already be members of an outdoor club. The large number of members vying for use of five or six rinks means that the relatively inexperienced player has very limited access to a rink and therefore lacks the opportunity for the frequent practice that he needs. By contrast, such opportunity was readily available on outdoor greens in the summer. The new player should first find his feet and gain experience and confidence before joining a private indoor club. This point was not known to me when I applied to join so that I found myself rather thrown in at the deep end. It was a case of either sink or swim. At least I had the correct dress, which is the same as for outdoor clubs.

One of my learned advisers subsequently put forward the other point of view, commenting, 'It is generally considered that an indoor club, whether private or municipal, is the best place to learn to play bowls as you do not have the same alterations in pace as outdoors, nor do you have to contend with appalling weather!'. This may be so, but my private club does not cater for the novice and I do not think it is alone in this respect. However, the indoor club offers perhaps the best opportunity to perfect one's game. I subsequently found that an associate member had a fair chance of having some games. The printed notice stated:

'Associate members, bowling facilities for members who are on the waiting list to become full playing members. The above may play –
   A   In the Sunday Mixed League
   B   The Christmas and Easter Mixed Tournament
   C   Spoon Drives if there is a vacancy
   D   Any session when there is a vacancy, providing he does not preclude a playing member from play and subject to previous approval of the green steward
   E   In a booked rink providing no playing member is deprived of a game.'

Not so long ago associate members were confined to a mere three games in any one season; today the situation is more relaxed and provided there is a vacancy one is encouraged to make up the numbers required to even up or fill a rink. I was advised that my best chance of getting a game would be to go along for the general lunchtime session. The club's playing day is divided up into six sessions: 09.30 to 11.00; 11.00 to 12.30; 12.30 to 14.30; 14.30 to 16.30; 16.30 to 19.00; 19.00 to 21.30. These timings vary slightly on Saturdays and Sundays. Not all these sessions are available for 'GP' (general play). Several may be allocated to matches, leagues or other organised events. The ladies also enjoy unrestricted use of the green on some days and times.

My first game, then, took place in the 12.30 pm general period on a Tuesday. I arrived at noon, because the rinks are made up prior to the appointed change-over time by the duty 'green ranger' or steward, to whom I was introduced by friends. He promised to try to fit me into a game. I was in luck, and was able to join a triples game. The six of us comprised five gentlemen and one lady, an experienced player who acted as skip for one team.

I have to admit that this game so far as I was concerned was a disaster. From my point of view the less said about it the better but, for the record, I just could not adjust my length to that demanded by an indoor rink. I had been told, no doubt by well-meaning people, that indoor carpets were always very fast and that my bowls would end up in the ditch until I became used to the non-grass surface. As this information was ingrained in my mind I found that my bowls reached little more than halfway up the rink! I was soon to learn that indoor rinks vary just as much as grassed lawns. My Worthing playing surface just happened to be one of the slowest known, averaging about 12 seconds, which is about the speed of most British outdoor greens. My team-mates were very kind and considerate, but it was obvious that I had spoiled the game for them.

A choice had to be made: to give up Indoor Bowls or to persevere and master the new conditions. I remembered Norman King's account of his introduction to the game as told in his helpful book *Tackle Bowls this Way*. 'Believe me', he says 'those woods were scattered around the green and were a shocking sight: they were everywhere. Personally, my dignity was very hurt by my inability to make those wood go anywhere near the spots I wanted them to finish and I decided there and then that they would not master me'.

I decided to go back to the club the following week to see if I could get in some much-needed practice. When I turned up there was Norman King himself, waiting to play in that session with some of his friends.

No doubt word had filtered through that my standard of play was well below par, for on hearing of my mission the green ranger explained to me that the members who had come along for this session were experienced players who normally arranged to play with their favourite team-mates, and that it might not be a good idea to break up their customary game. He suggested that I put my name down for the 'spoon match' that would follow at 2.30 pm. The list would be closed at 2.00 pm, and if there were any vacancies then, the associate members would be called upon to make up the required numbers of players. Because of its large membership, the Worthing club does not permit players to take part in consecutive sessions, so those who had played between 12.30 pm and 2.30 pm could not put their names down for the spoon match.

The term 'spoon match' was coined in the not-so-distant past, when silver-plated spoons complete with the club emblem cost a mere 35 pence, and were presented to members of the winning team. Vast collections could be built-up then, but today such trinkets cost about £3.00 and we are given instead vouchers for refreshments taken within the club.

The green ranger chooses from the list the players he considers most suitable to act as skips, and the remainder of the players are allocated their rinks by drawing lots.

Thus I came to play in my first spoon match. The beauty of such a game is that the players know in advance that the luck of the draw will bring up good players as well as novices so there are no hard feelings if someone like myself, having only his second indoor game, is introduced into the group.

We now had about 15 minutes to spare before the rink was ours at 2.30. We introduced ourselves and arranged an order of play for each team. I suggested that I should play lead as a beginner, but the captain wanted a more experienced player to take this position in order that our side might quickly establish a good position and hold shot wood. Consequently I was made number two and as such would have to keep the scorecard.

The initial preparation is especially important in indoor bowls for time is of the essence. As soon as one session ends at the ringing of a bell, so the next commences without interval. In order to save a few moments, it is the custom here for the jack to be placed in position by the captain of the leading side and not cast down the rink by the lead player. This convenient practice does not operate in serious matches where the full Laws of play apply.

I do not know if it was because of my more relaxed manner in the spoon match or on account of my mock deliveries in front of a mirror the night before, but truth to tell I did quite well in this my second indoor game. My length was greatly improved, my delivery more relaxed and correct, my line surprisingly good and I delivered quite a number of shot bowls. It was nice to know that the skip's congratulations were partly earned. I felt even more elated when the green master invited me to put my name down for a game the following week. I was rather glad I had decided to persevere.

One great surprise discovered in this first week was that, although all the rinks were under one roof in one large room with a continuous run of the same carpet, there were apparently changes in speed and running characteristics between the rinks and even between the ends on a single rink. These differences were admittedly slight and would not affect my game, but for those advanced players who wished to deliver a bowl with pinpoint accuracy, even these small variations are of importance. For example, one rink by a long north-facing window tends to run slower than the others because it is cooler in the winter. This difference cannot be more than a degree or so, depending on the outside temperature, but it is reflected in the speed of the carpet. The humidity, of course, affects the tautness of the carpet and therefore the speed of the bowls.

My second game was good experience for me, as in my outdoor Club the player of least ability played lead. The new position of number two meant that when I took my place on the mat there were already four or five bowls at the head. I now had to watch my captain and follow his instructions. In most cases, it was only a matter of being told to make a forehand or a backhand shot, perhaps to try to move an opponent's shot bowl or to ensure that I did not disturb one of our scoring bowls. It could also be that he wanted one of mine to be long so that we had a back wood should the skip decide, when his own turn came, to use a firing shot or otherwise run the jack back away from the other side's scoring bowls. As a lead I had been concerned only with delivering my bowls as near to the jack as possible. The skip seldom instructs the lead although he certainly should indicate his wishes to numbers two and three. These players must watch their captain and follow his signals which should be crystal clear.

I very much enjoyed my second game and resolved to try to fit in another spoon match at lunchtime the following week. During a working day, I thought, the relaxation and freedom from a constantly ringing phone would do me a power of good.

My third game was a slight anti-climax. I bowled reasonably well but no great improvement was evident. I think on reflection that I lacked wholehearted concentration. Perhaps I was a little too pleased with my previous game. One must keep on top and never let one's concentration wander. One new facet of indoor bowling came to light. We were playing six rinks to the green so that the different teams were rather close. It must be borne in mind too that on an indoor carpet it is usual to take a slightly wider green than on grass. When, therefore, I delivered one of my bowls with a wide forehand sweep, and a player on the next rink playing did exactly the same thing, in the reverse direction, our bowls were on a collision course and met with a resounding crash in the middle, each cannoning off across the green.

I, at least, remembered not to run after my stray shot – never run on a carpet. I learnt that such a crash was not all that rare indoors and that one was permitted to deliver the bowl again. In future I kept a weather eye open to ensure that a bowler on the next rink was not about to bowl into my path. One has to wait only a few seconds to avoid any risk of a clash. Bowls are apt to stray into the next rink in the normal run of their correct delivery. By the way, these indoor rinks do not have the taut green-string divisions found on outdoor greens.

The point about not running on an indoor bowling carpet is an important one. The large carpet is extremely expensive and must be treated with the utmost care. The extra jerky running steps and especially any sudden stop put a great strain on the fabric and may well ruck-up the underlay and result in a bumpy surface. The question of running has for long been a bone of contention in bowling circles but the 1986 edition of the World Indoor Bowls Council's Laws of the Game clearly state: 'It is the responsibility of all players, umpires and markers to refrain at all times from committing any act which is liable in any way to cause damage to the indoor green or carpet'.

You will also see large 'No smoking' notices prominently displayed. This usually forbids smoking only while on the carpet as ash can easily burn a hole in the expensive flooring. Personally, I would prefer it to be prohibited in the whole arena, as is the case in some clubs.

For my fourth attempt to join an indoor game, I tried a spoon match session held on Tuesday morning. I was not able to play as the maximum number, all full playing members, had already put their names on the list. I was, however, now free to sit awhile and observe the play of those already on the green and those who replaced them when the spoon competition started.

This observation was quite interesting. My original idea was to watch the line or green taken by the experienced bowlers who were accustomed to the indoor carpet. I soon changed to watching the grips, the stance on the mat and the delivery. I was most surprised by the very high number of foot faults. The Laws for both indoor and outdoor games are basically the same and are quite clear as to the position of the feet or one foot at the time of delivery: 'A player . . . at the moment of delivering the jack or his bowl, shall have one foot remaining entirely within the confines of the mat. The foot may be either in contact with, or over the mat. Failure to observe this law constitutes foot faulting'.

However, several experienced players had little more than a toe or heel on or over the mat. This may not be checked or even mentioned in a friendly internal club game, but once one drifts into bad habits they tend to stick and can lead to embarrassing comment in more important matches. I am not for a moment suggesting that these players were cheating in any way – to be a few inches up the rink is not of great consequence. They were merely being rather careless in this regard and were probably quite unaware that they were at fault. I only make the point so that new players will be more careful and ensure that their stance on the mat is correct. It is after all the easiest part of the bowling art.

I also had the opportunity of studying the delivery, which varied greatly from player to player. Many, far too many, bowls were delivered on too narrow a grass-line, that is the running line of the bowl was too straight taking little account of the bias. This was because the whole body was not at the required angle, the feet were facing the front as were the shoulders. The player then sought to swing the bowl across his body. This gives a very variable result and is therefore not to be recommended. Some of those who did stand at the correct angle then tend to place the left foot straight down the rink as they delivered the bowl. That steadying left foot should follow the angle of the body, a quarter right for a forehand shot or a quarter (or so) left for the backhand. Most deliveries were consequently too narrow rather than too wide. Of course, many of the deliveries were good, no doubt the result of sound coaching and constant practice so that the correct stance and the smooth delivery were second nature to that bowler.

It also surprised me how many of these experienced players flicked the arm or wrist away to the left as they completed the delivery. The bowl may already have left their hand but that follow-through should be a straight one, deviating not to the left or right. Yet some seemed to swing a couple of feet or more out of the correct path. Having observed these faulty deliveries I am able to take care not to fall into the same slack

Above and below. *A text-book back hand delivery at the Gateway Masters. Recording the TV coverage can reveal perfect stance, delivery and follow-through, as well as highlight faults from different angles.*

practices myself. It is useful to be able to learn from other people's mistakes.

Another practice that I think would be frowned on in important games was wide-spread: starting to gather up the bowls in the completed head before the score had been agreed or some measure taken. It certainly saves valuable time in club games to gather in the obviously non-scoring shots, but what if you knock one on to the jack or on to a bowl that has to be measured?

I may sound like a barrack-room lawyer, but I am trying to spotlight common faults so that they will not be made when it really matters.

My next game, my fifth, was an early morning one. Even so, others before me in the line had put their names down for lead and number two, so I found myself as number three, and out of my depth again! I obviously had to bowl into a head which already held at least eight woods (we were playing a foursome) and had to obey my skip's instructions as to the playing hand, weight, and so forth. I must say I didn't do at all badly, or at least I kept my end up with the other early-morning players!

One member of our team did, however, get rather upset when the skip asked him to bowl on his forehand. A lead is normally left to deliver in his own way, just so long as his woods end up near the jack, and this player was accustomed to employing a backhand delivery. He was quite cross with the skip for changing his style and this affected his delivery for some time. I only make this point to illustrate the value of a quiet word with the skip before the game. However, you should really be able to bowl either forehand or backhand. If you are weak on one then take the trouble to practise.

Although I was at last bowling reasonably well, I was not able to be a very helpful aide to my skip when I was standing at the head and the two skips took up their delivery positions at the far end of the rink. One of my great difficulties was that I did not know which of the delivered woods belonged to our team and which to the other side. I knew my own bowls, but that was about all. The number three must of course know exactly the state of the score, which woods need to be 'taken out' by the skip and which are his own side's and, as such, should be left. Luckily my skip did not need my advice!

I know now that the number three should check all the bowls belonging to his team and memorise or take note of their individual symbols. In a serious club or county game the team's bowls will carry special identification labels and no difficulty should arise.

The same basic difficulty, however, arose when we came to agree the score. Neither I nor my opposite number were really clear as to the ownership of all the woods. We had to ask 'Whose bowl is that?'. A waste of valuable time and a great embarrassment. Before you condemn us too much, remember that there are over 500 members in the club plus all the associates and, in my case at least, I had never played with any of these people before and had never seen their unmarked bowls.

We started the game without a measure (I had one on my Christmas list but this festival was three weeks ahead), a lapse which caused even more embarrassment. Most experienced players are very good judges of distance when the score is being agreed, but the eye can be somewhat prejudiced, especially when the 'old soldier' is aware that he is up against a mere rookie who will be unlikely to argue a point. The new player should be a little on his guard against being leaned upon by a more experienced bowler when the count is being agreed. He may be an inexperienced player but he need not necessarily be naive! A friendly question or a suggestion that the distances be measured should soon show that you are not to be browbeaten. You might be well advised to watch the measuring, too. I get the impression, probably quite incorrectly, that this measuring and the count can be quite a duel between the two number threes.

My next game was a very happy affair well suited to the pre-Christmas period. The

A local member who has to use the semi-fixed stance – to very good effect.

conversations were very friendly and I was receiving much encouragement and advice. I still needed such help as far too many of my woods were going astray. One had an extremely serious bout of wobbles – I made a mental note to watch that grip and to keep my little finger off the side of the bowl. Still, it was an excellent, well-balanced game which we won by one point. My first indoor win.

The off-rink conversation between the two leads, of whom I was one, brought to my attention the mass of talent we had on the green. There was a Squadron-Leader, another player who had survived the siege of Malta, another who had been in the Dambuster Squadron, and others with various doubtless well-earned decorations. These luminaries were, however, equal on the carpet with the most humble soul – even with me, a mere ex-Corporal! We were on first name terms, all fellow bowlers, all equal members of a club.

What was more remarkable was the fact that some were disabled in some way or another, perhaps by war wounds. One club member has a wooden leg although spectators would not be aware of his handicap. Another has lost an arm, yet he has a remarkably balanced delivery. Other players are past the age when mobile sports would seem practicable. Yet all are able to play on equal terms, or very nearly so, with the more fortunate of us. Their stance on the mat and their delivery may of necessity be unique and they may bump the bowl down rather heavily on the carpet, but the woods are placed with remarkable accuracy and they are enjoying the game as much as or even more than the rest of us. Bowling is a great leveller. Even the blind can play a good game, although they obviously need some special aids. The Worthing Council have even specially adapted one outdoor green to enable those confined to a wheelchair to enjoy bowling.

Some seven and a half months since I first stepped on to a green I played my seventh indoor game, a red-letter day, one of my shots being described as 'brilliant'. 'Fluke' may have been a better description, or one that I shall use until I can get all my woods within a foot of the jack. The odd one is certainly not good enough. Still, it is surprising how I was coming on with practice. I still have difficulty in controlling length, so I must work on this aspect of the delivery. However, even the world champions have the same trouble.

I mentioned just now friendly conversations on the rink. Some eyebrows may well have been raised at this for chatter can break not only your concentration but that of the person on the mat preparing to bowl. One would not engage in such general conversations in an important match: our game was purely a friendly affair – almost a roll-up – but nevertheless our talk was in the main confined to the time when we were walking up the rink and awaiting the turn of the skips to bowl. The layout of our indoor club also permits and indeed encourages players to sit out at the raised end of the green or on the wide sidewalk which is equipped with chairs and tables. The leads and, to a lesser degree, the number twos can therefore sit down after they have delivered their woods and engage in friendly discussion.

A dedicated player in an important match would no doubt prefer to remain on the carpet, the better to watch every delivery and the position of all the woods as they arrive at the head. We, on a lesser level, can normally catch up when we take our place there. The question of resting and sitting is one that troubles many. Roy Downing told me off in no uncertain terms on the first day he coached me, stating that we would not sit down unless we were feeling ill. He further added that County selectors would never pick a player whom they observed sitting on the bank or on a chair off the green.

The opposite view is taken by some leading players, even when taking part in an important match. They make the valid point that bowls, especially in long matches and particularly for the more elderly, can be a tiring game and that it can be advantageous and beneficial to take an occasional rest and so take the weight off one's feet. Personally, I will continue to take an occasional rest. This must not be taken to mean that one can leave the playing area (certainly not without the permission of the skip) or lose concentration to the extent of not being ready when it is your turn to bowl. I am talking of a revitalising rest, not a doze! After all, champion billiards players sit in their corners smoking or sipping their drinks when they are not at the table. Still, if sitting is taboo at your club, it is best for it to be taboo for you also.

At 8.30 am on Christmas Eve I joined others in a queue outside the club hoping that I would get a game. As it happened there were five other associates who had been able to escape pre-Christmas duties, so six of us played a triples game together. We all played remarkably well and the heads looked much better and more compact than some of those formed by some club members with far more experience. We were also reasonably equally balanced although this fact was not reflected in the score, 17 to 2. My side went ten ends before scoring a single point!

The trouble was one skip who had the edge on us all. Time and again my holding shot woods were taken out by the skip or the jack was trailed back to one of his back woods. It was a good-humoured game and the opposition readily admitted that we were just not having our share of luck. It was not so much luck as unbalanced captaincy. One was a good bowler able to plan the head and capable of taking advantage of the opportunities offered. Ours had been pressed into the position and was rather out of his depth, a feeling which I know only too well. He gave us very little instruction and his last two shots were so seldom able to score. This experience shows how important good skipping is and how it can swing a game or a match.

This very important aspect of the game was further demonstrated when, as this game finished, I was asked to make up a triples in the next session. My skip now was a younger player with six years' experience. He had risen quickly from lead to skip and had studied not only the game but also the craft of the skip. He was very keen. As with the previous game, the first four players were extremely evenly balanced, but this time the scores were practically reversed. The new skip made all the difference.

He did not just stand at the head. Once I had got an early bowl somewhere near the jack he stepped in to take command. He signalled clearly with his duster exactly where he wanted my next wood. I, as lead, had never been so taken in hand before, always having been left to do my basic duty of drawing to the jack. Here I was placing a back wood at what was to me a strangely early period of the game. Similarly, the number two received explicit instructions. As a result, we all rose to the occasion and his claps and praise were well-earned.

To add to our good fortune he was an expert bowler himself and so was well able to repair any errors we had made and to cancel out the often excellent shots of the other skip. We by no means had a walkover, but we had been lifted by our skip who very obviously knew his job and was able to instruct us in a clear manner.

These two Christmas Eve games were highly instructive to me. I learned much about skipping and indeed that scores do not reflect the amount of enjoyment that both sides derive from participating in the game. There has, I suppose, to be a score and a result, but these are really incidentals in a club game.

After this game the skip, whom I had not previously met, congratulated me on my accuracy and asked how long I had been playing. I in turn was able to say how much we had enjoyed the game and benefited from his leadership. He explained how he had felt when he started as a lead, having received no instruction whatsoever. He now sought to remedy this deficiency – to learn from other's mistakes.

In my next game I was, for the first time indoors, able to use my full set of four bowls as I was lucky enough to be included in a pairs game. Play was enjoyable, if unremarkable. We were all evenly matched associate members endeavouring to work off Christmas excesses. Two points arose from this game. We decided to swap positions at the halfway stage, the leads becoming skips and vice versa. This was good and gave us all some (much needed) experience of directing from the head, but remember this cannot be done in a serious game played under the Laws of the game which very clearly state that the playing positions cannot be changed once the game has commenced.

Also one skip happened to notice that another's bowls did not bear a valid year-stamp. Once again this does not matter in a club roll-up or minor game but, if that player only owns the one set, he may be in serious trouble if asked to play in an important match. He might well have to borrow an in-date set which would be unfamiliar. His old accustomed set can be re-tested and re-stamped, but the time to have this done is now! An EBA ruling at the end of 1985 dispensed with re-stamping from the beginning of 1986, which means that bowls bearing a 1985 or later stamp can continue to be used until the stamp becomes illegible. One should note that the stamped year numbers should be legible and that this concession relates only to competitive and domestic play in England. International events are governed by other regulations as decreed by other national or international associations.

Having finished this welcome pairs game I came across another associate member who had been unable to get a game in the first session and unfortunately had not been picked for the second session either. As there was a rink available I asked him if he would like to have an hour's game with me. I therefore not only did him a good turn but was able to play my first indoor singles game. Once more all four bowls were in use which makes for good practice. The first short delivery may be excusable but you should be able to increase the run with the next. If you then overdo the correction, you have a third and a fourth bowl to perfect your delivery.

We decided to play sets as in tennis, which is often done in televised bowls games. In this scoring system, the first player to reach seven shots wins the set and you re-start, continuing thus until an agreed number of sets has been played. For a short game, one would play the best of three sets. This system tends to even out the score and perhaps reflects better the talents of the two players. A 21-9 result may suggest unevenly matched opponents but, in fact, one player may just have had a little more luck than the other in swinging a few ends by the delivery of his last wood. A game is never won or lost until the last bowl has come to rest, so never give up. John and I had a great hour together. We varied the length of the jack from extremely short to very long and played good, enjoyable bowls. I was very surprised at the end of the game to learn that he had taken it up only five months previously. Perhaps I should not have been surprised, for he had hung about for over two hours waiting for the chance of a game and was obviously dedicated and keen to gain experience and practice.

The last game of my first calendar year was on 31 December. I need only record four of my errors in the hope that they will not be emulated. The green was crowded, six rinks were in use, each with its full complement of eight bowlers. At the start the mats were all placed at the regulation distance, which left only four feet or less in which the players could stand, with 16 bowls lying about. Having delivered my first shot, I stepped back, still looking at the path of my bowl. I stumbled and all but fell over a group of these woods just behind me. A fellow player said he had fallen and broken his wrist in similar circumstances. Moral: never step back without first looking to see whether the carpet is clear of obstructions.

My second, minor, error was occasioned by the same crowded conditions. As we walked up to the head and met the two skips returning in the opposite direction, I stepped across to my right to make room for the skip and nearly impeded a bowl delivered on the next rink. There were great shouts and the wood missed my feet by less than half an inch. Moral: when walking up the rink keep in a tight bunch or walk in single file.

On the second end, when I still was not sure of the ownership of the various bowls, I had it in mind that we had won the end. I therefore placed the mat, proceeded to take up my stance and then delivered a beauty which nestled right up to the jack. Only then did someone point out that I had gone out of turn – we had lost the last end. My toucher had to be returned and we re-started the game, much to my distress.

My last error of the year was the most serious and one of which I have already forewarned you. In my haste (this word should not be in the bowler's vocabulary) to progress I started kicking in the bowls at the head, thinking that the score had been agreed. Two points had been but the number threes were about to measure for a third point. The fact that I kicked this contested wood away meant, of course, that we had to concede the point.

Not a good result for my last game of the year. Four New Year's resolutions presented themselves! Eager to put them into practice, I went to the club on New Year's Day. There was a spare rink which I took for the session. I had for the previous few months wondered how I could get in some solo practice, and this modest investment proved to be an extremely good one.

I practised casting an indoor jack, my first opportunity as in the club games it has always been placed by the skip. I discovered its strangely heavy indoor weight and found I could control the distance quite well. Having the rink to myself I could use four bowls. I alternated between short and very long jacks. I could and did experiment with different standing positions on the mat. I surprised myself by my better than average accuracy in drawing to the jack. This was probably because I was able to concentrate, I could use my first bowl for ranging purposes and above all I did not feel hurried. I took careful aim at the corner peg. I studied my delivery and follow-through. I checked the position of my feet. I enjoyed myself and treated myself to two coffee breaks.

I purposely practised with short jacks and the mat placed well up the rink. I found that this rather suited my delivery – there was no need to force the shot to achieve a lengthy run. I probably bowled more woods in that hour and a half than I had in all my fours games since I joined the club. I was sure the practise did me the world of good and resolved to make such solo sessions part of my practice routine.

Afterwards I was able to join a triples game. I acted as lead – this was to be my position for at least another season, until I had enough experience of other required shots and more knowledge of tactics.

For the first six or seven ends, the luck did not seem to be with us. We held good shots only to lose them to the last opposing wood. We trailed by ten or so, and then suddenly we held a shot, won the end and I had possession of the mat.

Obviously, I opted for a short jack with the mat well up – a most welcome change from the long jacks the other side favoured. My earlier practice session certainly paid dividends. I bowled beautifully to this shorter distance. We won six points at one end and did not look back. It is remarkable how a good end can lift a losing team and how a change of tactics can swing its fortunes. In the last end I achieved two nudging touchers, woods that just trickle up to the jack, touch it but do not roll on, to be all but useless. These two dead-length shots were just about perfection for line and length and they remained untouched to gain two shots. We won the game by five or six points.

Thus the year started well: good practice and a pleasingly successful, cheerful game, with none of the silly errors I had made only the previous day. It is strange how one's play can swing like this. Luck you may say: I put it down to practice and rather more concentration than I am normally able to command.

I was quite amazed by the progress I made in a few weeks from that first really disastrous indoor game in which all my bowls were stranded half way up the rink.

On one occasion at the club I sat and studied the performance of one player – Norman King, the former international. How sweetly he bowled, what poise, what balance, what accuracy! How could I ever begin to emulate this beautiful action? David Bryant has said: 'King is as sweet as anyone in getting his bowls away'. This is still true today. Now in his 70s, he is to be seen most lunchtimes playing a friendly fours – not, I might add, with other internationals or even with County players, but with ordinary club members, all merely seeking an enjoyable game. He now puts up with me each Tuesday lunchtime.

Norman King came into bowls after football, and like most of us made a dismal display at first. He persevered and reached the very top, which is encouraging for us all.

Norman King demonstrating a perfect text-book style action to Roy Downing's students. Try to copy this before you go your own individual way!

Many internal and inter-club events are held at the club. Each Wednesday, Saturday and Sunday at least one and often two matches take place. I have taken the trouble to watch several of these contests and to have witnessed the good spirit in which they are conducted. Although as I am still an associate member I am not yet permitted to represent the club in matches, I hope in the future to be able to participate in some of them.

I have taken to visiting the club on a Saturday or Sunday evening for the general sessions. I have been pleased to see that most of these games are of a mixed nature, indeed more women seem to be on the rinks than men. I played in one game recently with another gentleman and four ladies. On balance they out-bowled us both, and one lady in particular was brilliant, but more importantly we all thoroughly enjoyed the evening.

I must record that as a mere associate member I have not by any means been made to feel a second-class citizen. The club captain and the duty green stewards have all been extremely helpful and have made every endeavour to give me a game within the club rules, finding an extra player when I was left as an odd-man-out or even rearranging the green to take six rinks rather than the normal and much more comfortable five. What more can an associate paying a reduced subscription ask for. Well, I have got more, for on two occasions full members have stepped down to offer their places in a game to me. This is true club spirit – the spirit of bowls. I should add that I have kept the preparation of this published account completely to myself. Nobody within the club had an inkling that I was writing of my experiences, so their helpfulness was completely genuine.

In casual conversations I have discovered that many players prefer the indoor greens to the summer outdoor game. They give several valid reasons for this preference. The games are not dependent on the weather, on light or indeed on the condition of the green. The indoor facilities are available whatever the outside weather for 12 hours a day. Because the carpet 'green' is reasonably constant, by and large the bowl will end up where you put it. A bad shot must be blamed on your technique not on the green, and beautiful deliveries can more often be credited to good judgement rather than luck. There is, for example, no wind to help or hinder.

Indoor clubs also provide a warm haven with good facilities for refreshments both solid and liquid. Most clubs will provide pleasant viewing-areas and even reading-rooms with daily newspapers and the bowling magazines. We can also sit and watch television. It can almost be described as a home from home. An added bonus is the fact that an indoor club attracts members from a dozen or more outdoor clubs and one can consequently make many new friends.

It is not surprising, then, that so many new Indoor Bowls Clubs are being formed or that bowling greens are being provided by sports centres. While it is not the case with my private indoor club in Worthing, several such indoor greens are open all the year round, so that it is not really a winter addition to a summer game but a recommended aspect of the year-round sport.

The popular television coverage of indoor bowls tournaments will doubtless add to the demand for such facilities, encouraging the indoor clubs and the municipal greens to cater for the new bowler as well as the experienced player.

The first book to be devoted to the indoor game was Arthur Sweeney's *Indoor Bowls* (Nicholas Kaye, London), which was published in 1966. This experienced author gives in this pioneer work details of the cost then of building indoor greens, their care and maintenance as well as useful details of the game and its mode of play. As I write Arthur Sweeney is still playing in the West Country; he will be 90 in September. Arthur was secretary of the English Indoor Bowling Association and has done much for indoor bowling in this country.

Perhaps, in view of the high cost of providing large indoor greens with six or more regulation-size rinks, the small-scale Short-Mat game will become the means of training and attracting to the game new bowlers, in particular the younger player. Short-Mat facilities can be provided at relatively little cost in hotels, small sports centres or large public houses. The Short-Mat Bowls Association is now an associate member of the English Indoor Bowling Association.

Short-Mat Bowls

When I first took up bowls I thought there was but one version – the outdoor Lawn Bowls game as played on my local greens during the summer months. Then, as recounted in the last chapter, I discovered the indoor game, which takes the sport through the winter months. Next I learned of local variations such as the Federation game, which is played in and around East Anglia, and, of course, the Crown Green game. Subsequently I read the brief reports of the Short-Mat game published in the two bowls magazines.

I experienced great difficulty in learning about this version and about the whereabouts of Short-Mat clubs in Sussex. In my own outdoor and indoor clubs not one word was mentioned of short mats and I deduced that none of our serious players had dabbled in this mini-game. Yet this infant is extremely strong and promises to grow apace and to lead many of its followers into the wider field of bowls.

I decided to join a mid-week bowling break at the Ocean Hotel at Saltdean near Brighton to gain an insight into the new game and perhaps to write it off in a paragraph or two as a pub-type game played by teenagers.

The event was sponsored by Butlin's Hotels who offered 'over £2,000 in cash and holidays' to the winners of the main events – mens' singles, ladies' singles and mixed pairs.

The hotel's standard charge for the four days in 1986 was a modest £65 per person, plus VAT. This included the bowling sessions, full board and access to other Butlins amenities which included the pool complex, table tennis and billiards. Several family groups were present and the young children seemed well occupied and amused with the non-bowling events. In addition, group discounts were available for parties of 12 or more.

By 'short mat' we mean a strip measuring in length between the maximum permitted 45 feet and the minimum 40 feet. Those used at the Butlin's event were 45 feet long. The width is a mere 6 feet with a permitted tolerance of two inches to allow for the metric equivalent of the standard British measurements. The mats used at the Butlin's hotel were Wilton bowling felt as supplied by the Lodge Sports Shop in Stickford, Lincolnshire, but, as with other items of bowling equipment, there are various makers and suppliers most of whom advertise regularly in the bowls magazines. One other short mat is Regalgrene, made by Messrs Bury Cooper Whitehead Ltd of Bury, Lancashire, a firm which has been most helpful to me. These mats, eight in number, were laid out in the hotel ballroom. Three were on the uncarpeted dancing area, five on the thickly-carpeted surround. Those laid on the wood obviously gave a faster surface than those on the carpet, which acted as an extra underlay. This difference, while not ideal, did not seem to create any great difficulty for the players. More serious were the slight uneven-nesses in the floor and therefore in the playing surface.

The layout or marking of the short mat will surprise players of the conventional game. The first great difference is that a white, wooden bar or 'block' straddles the centre line. This centrally-placed block is 15 inches long, leaving only 28½ inches each side of the block for your grass-line. The main purpose of the block is to stop firing shots being projected all around the room. The block and the short run to the jack, which will be between 38 and 41 feet from the end fender (or from 36 to 39 feet from the front of the mat) ensures that the game calls for finesse rather than brute force. This surely is one of the attractions of the game. Few players can claim to be unable to roll a bowl some 33 feet.

The end-markings on the short mat are unique to this variation of the game but should not be off-putting for any player. The wooden fender of 3 × 3-inch timber surrounds each end of the mat, enclosing the ditch, which is not recessed. The mat is placed up against the fender within the marked lines in the ditch area. It is always placed in the same position and cannot be moved, even forward.

On each side of the mat are white delivery lines. These are 13 inches out from the central line or, if you prefer, 23 inches from the side of the mat. As the name implies, your feet must not touch or cross either of these lines as you make your delivery. As always, at least one foot must be completely on or over the mat as the bowl is delivered. You will also notice a central line some three feet up the rink. This is disregarded when delivering – it is the jack line marked at each end of the playing surface. The jack is placed on this line at the far end of the rink, its position on the central line being dictated by the person or team winning the previous end.

You will also notice a line across the rink six feet up from the far ditch line. This is the dead line and any bowl not completely passing this line must be removed from the carpet and placed behind the far fender. Likewise, a bowl touching or knocking over the block is dead and its further progress up the rink must be stopped before it runs into the head or any live wood. The block is, of course, reset in its original position which will be indicated by a short, white line marked on the mat.

Play progresses in the normal manner using standard-size bowls, normally of number 3 bias. There is no need to buy special equipment for the Short-Mat game. Although this contest was restricted to singles and doubles games, both triples and fours can be played on the short mat – with fours, though, the head would be very crowded with bowls.

The commencing lead and subsequent winners have the jack placed on the jack line at a length to suit their preference. The stance on the mat, grip and delivery are as described earlier for Lawn or Indoor bowling except that little or no back-swing is required as you need only gently roll the bowl some 30 feet. A bowl delivered by a person guilty of foot-faulting should be stopped by the marker and considered dead.

A sound basic delivery is called for as the grass-line is very limited. If you over-grass the bowl will leave the mat, if you take too narrow a line you will hit the block. In both cases the bowl is dead. If you bowl too short you will not clear the dead line, too long and you will be in the ditch. Nevertheless, it is surprisingly easy to acquire the required touch. With no previous experience of playing on a short mat, I was sending up quite reasonable woods after six or seven deliveries and even had two touchers within five minutes. The same rules apply relating to the toucher remaining live when ditched.

Above. *The short-mat markings and fenders. The white block is in position and the jack is on its line.*

Left. *As in outside games the jack may be knocked or trailed from its original central position. Play continues to the off-centre jack – not so easy with the block in position.*

While I found it easy to adjust my delivery to the Short-Mat game, I found it much harder later in the week to revert to a good length on the full-size rink, which is double the length of the one on which I had been playing at Butlin's.

I took part in a mixed doubles event on the Wednesday morning. Much to my surprise, my partner and I handsomely won the first round – my first Short-Mat game. We were well away in the second game and were leading our strong and practised opponents 5-0 when they won an end and elected to play to a long jack. 'Long' here is relative, for the jack line is only 36 inches long; but that extra three feet seemed to make all the difference and we went six ends without scoring a single point. Yes, just as in the full size rink, tactics and good skipping certainly play their part on the short mat. I felt a little happier about the defeat when the pair went on through the rounds to reach the semi-finals.

In this reasonably informal event we played in timed sessions of 30 minutes, which eased the organiser's timing problems considerably. If the scores were even when the time was up, a deciding end was played. On more formal occasions a pre-decided number of ends would be played, perhaps preceded by one or two trials ends. While the games were played to English Short-Mat Bowling Association rules, the event cannot be considered to be controlled by that Association as qualified umpires were not officiating.

Apart from the standard games we also played target bowls. Here a circular plastic-coated cloth target some four feet in diameter was placed with its centre on a long jack position. I paced the direct distance as 14 yards from the front of the mat. The central 'bullseye' section had a diameter of 9¾ inches and a bowl resting in this all-too-small area scored ten points. Around this were four concentric bands 4½ inches wide with the following values: 5, 3, 2 and 1 for the outer ring.

The object is of course to bowl your four woods to rest on the target as near the centre as possible. It sounds very simple but is surprisingly difficult. Even experienced players need all their skill to rest all four bowls on the target. My best effort after 20 minutes or so was to score 26 points; two tens, a five and an outer. The highest possible score is 40, but you would need not only skill but also plenty of luck to rest all four bowls in the bullseye. In our target tournament the players were required to progress around four targets on different mats with slightly different speeds and characteristics. The player with the highest score from the 16 bowls won a free holiday. For the record, the winning score was 71.

Our mode of play was the simplest. If you wish to make the contest more difficult you can play against an opponent rather than on your own. Apart from the fact that eight bowls may arrive on the target, your opposite number could easily knock your good scoring bowls off the target with a good firing shot, thereby reducing your score of 30 or so to nil. This is possible as the block is not used in target bowls. You will find that in general it is better to have short bowls that can be promoted onwards rather than long shots which tend to be knocked off the end.

The use of these targets was good fun – perhaps more suited to an enjoyable evening's sport rather than a serious club event – but is is certainly an interesting variation on the standard game. You can also, if you so wish, use the target on a full-size rink where the greater distance between the mat and the target makes the task more difficult.

As for the Laws of the Short-Mat game, there are few amendments to the standard outdoor form. One important difference is that whereas in conventional games a jack or bowl has to cross a line entirely to be dead or out of play, in the Short-Mat game it has only to touch or partly cross the line to become dead.

Above. *The target placed on the short mat in the jack's position. It is surprisingly difficult to rest your bowls in the inner rings.*

Left. *The measure comes into play. Note the dead bowl placed behind the end fender.*

You should also watch the following points. You must not follow your bowl up the rink either on the mat or alongside it, and you must not deliver your bowl until the preceding one has come to rest. Infringement of either Law constitutes a fault and your bowls should be stopped and declared dead, except in the case of following up, where the first offence should warrant only a warning. In team events it is permissible to change the order of the players after the completion of any end, which is not the case in other non-Federation games. Also, practice on the mat prior to a game seems to be allowed.

The Short-Mat game is a serious one and no mere home game to be played in the drawing-room at Christmas! Having established the nature of the game with its British regional associations (the Welsh being senior in the date of establishment) and its published Laws, it can also rightly be stated that it will suit all ages and types of players. This mid-week event in Sussex attracted players from Wales, Devon and Shropshire as well as many from the London area. In age they ranged from 24 to 77, and they all enjoyed themselves. Many were having practice roll-ups before breakfast and were at it again after dinner! Several came as family groups while some couples booked in together, presumably having travelled down to have a pleasant break in Sussex. Despite the many rival attractions in Brighton all the bowlers remained in the rather hot ballroom watching the games and inspiring the players.

No acknowledged national player was present as a competitor although the youngest player was the son of a Welsh international lady bowler. No doubt some professionals may now or in the future try their skill on the short mat. In fact their presence at Butlin's might have spoilt the family atmosphere of the occasion. There were no firm favourites and everybody was in with a good chance of winning the numerous trophies and prizes on offer.

While Butlin's sponsored the bowling tournament, the arrangement and control of play was rightly in the hands of a professional – Chris Mills, the editor of *Bowls International,* who started the series for Butlin's at the Blackpool Metropole in February 1985. Chris is helped by various well-known and experienced players who act as umpires. In the main the markers are volunteers from among the competitors who happen not to be engaged in that match. The arrangement and control of the games seemed to be extremely well organised, the games and sessions flowing on in a very friendly fashion without hitch. It was a pleasing and instructive introduction to the Short-Mat game which, with its relatively cheap mats and the small playing area required, must surely spread quickly in England. I understand it is already popular in Wales and Ireland, and has been for a number of years.

On reflection it seems that the spread of this handy and inexpensive version of the game would be well-served if similar events were held for the novice, giving some basic instruction in the art of bowling. If you can learn your stance, grip and delivery on the short mat and deliver bowls within the narrow confines permitted you should have no fears on full-size rinks. I understand that the Worthing Corporation has now introduced Short-Mat bowling at our Sports Centre and that such tuition is given.

For those contemplating buying Short-Mat bowling equipment – and such complete sets are now readily available – for personal or club use, I would point out that one needs a flat surface as the mat and its bonded base are uniform and will not rectify any unevenness in the under-surface. You will also need space surrounding the mat to enable the players to stand behind the fender before bowling or while acting as skip at the far end. You will need to be able to walk around the mat – an extra two yards would not be unreasonable.

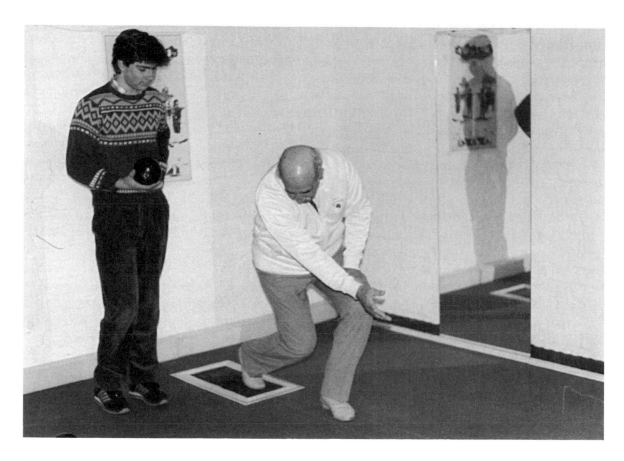

Above. *Roy Downing demonstrating the delivery to Jonathan who is about to test a set of bowls on this practice rink.*
Below. *The curved end of the practice rink which returns the bowl to the bowler.*

There is an even smaller version of the game, or rather a method of practising delivery, that you can use within your own home. I refer here to a bowls practice board which I have just seen in Roy Downing's Worthing shop. This apparatus, which was priced at under £50 in 1986, comprises a curved ramp with various markings indicating how far up the ramp a short, medium or long delivery would climb before stopping and rolling back to the player. It is said that only 12 feet of space is required and that the device will enable the player to perfect his delivery. It may well be helpful in that the delivered bowl is returned to the player, but the home carpet and the narrow ramp can hardly have the same speed as the playing rink. I would have thought that such a small apparatus would make you tend to bowl narrow rather than take the line that you will need when playing on a full-size rink.

Television and Video Recordings as an Aid to Your Play

With modern technology it is possible to have the cream of world bowlers practically playing in your own home or on your lawn. Of course, you do need access to a video cassette recorder. Purchasing mine was one of the best investments I have ever made. Not only can we record educational programmes for our son long after he has gone to bed or while he is at school, and our own favourite programmes, but as an added bonus I can record leading bowlers at both indoor and outdoor tournaments to watch and study at my leisure. I must make it clear that in recording these copyright-protected programmes I am doing so solely to watch in my own home with my own family – it would be quite wrong and unlawful to use these recordings for commercial purposes. It may well be that in time the television companies will issue their own cassettes of the major bowling events; in the meantime one has to record one's own or purchase other's edited highlights.

It is interesting to view the bowl's progress from different angles, some shots being taken from a camera giving an aerial view that no one present around the green could hope to approach. You can clearly see how each bowl travels almost straight along its line of delivery for the first three-fifths of its path and how, as it loses speed, the bias comes into play and the curve becomes greater and greater as it trickles to a stop. When playing back a video recording, one can of course slow down the action, stop the picture at a particular point or even, on modern machines, reverse the action so that the bowl runs back from the jack up the rink into the bowler's hand. These facilities can be extremely instructive.

The next moment one is treated to a close-up of a master bowler's delivery. How smooth and balanced it appears! Sometimes one has a side-on view, at other times from straight down the rink in line with the jack. No side swing or flick of the wrist is to be seen. You can see, however, that some players favour a straighter-running bowl than other players. Watching Tony Allcock and John Bell, it is clear that Allcock's has less bias. It will, of course, be within the permitted limits. World bowlers of this calibre will have several sets of bowls to suit various conditions or speeds of the greens. Much may depend on choosing the right set for, unlike a racing driver and his tyres, the bowler cannot change his choice during the match.

It is encouraging for the beginner to see that even these experts, who must spend the better part of each year on a green, do not always manage to reach the jack or even leave their bowl within a couple of feet of the target. Do not get me wrong, more often than

This sequence shows Jonathan making a good draw to the jack. Note not only the path of his bowl but that he stands in front of the mat watching for any further correction of line or length.

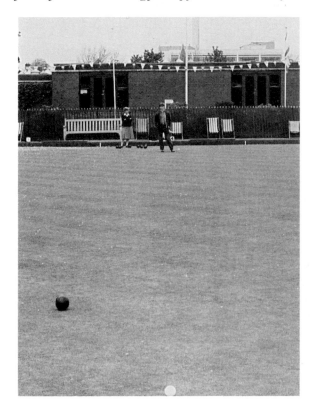

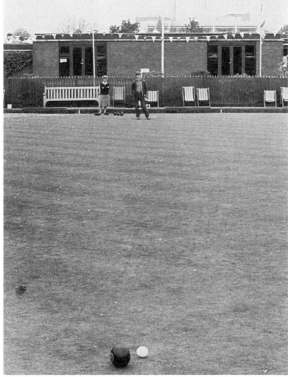

not they bowl to within a very few inches of the jack or their other intended spot. But it is a matter of 90 rather than 100 per cent accuracy. It is also encouraging for me and all those of slightish stature that you do not have be a six-foot giant to be up with the world's leading bowlers. My video recording of the 1986 Gateway Masters tournament shows Canadian Ron Jones playing John Bell, who must tower 12 inches or so over little Ron. For those who may have watched this very close match, Ron Jones was the busy chap in a red feathered Canada cap who seemed to spend must of the time polishing his bowls. Usually Ron ends the delivery low down resting his left knee on the grass in front of the mat. In this way he can sight the grass-line of his bowl as it travels up the green.

The commentary is just right. David Vine (with David Rhys Jones) offers some explanation regarding the tactics and the score with added valid comments and analysis of the play. It is interesting to note how frequently fortunes change in the scoring of each end and certainly as the whole game progresses. An end or a game is not won until the very last bowl comes to a stop, so keep pegging away – your play may suddenly become inspired. Your opponent may get careless or over-confident. One lucky shot or 'wick' can easily swing the whole game your way. You will never see a good experienced player give up trying, he will play his best to the very last. Nothing is certain; once you win an end by a single shot you have possession of the jack and are back in command – or should be!

One example of a dramatic victory against all odds, on the last end, is featured on my 1986 Gateway Masters recording. It starts with Tony Allcock standing at 20 points, one

Not all players follow the book. Here you see David Bryant in a typical delivery pose. A very good follow-through, with one foot entirely over the mat as the bowl is delivered.

short of the required winning total of 21. Ron Jones has scored only 17 and therefore needs a full house of all his four woods in scoring positions to reach the target. This seems impossible with two such evenly matched world–class bowlers. Yet Ron achieves a maximum score on the last end with a neat trail of the jack on his last delivery. All the Canadian's woods are now nearer the jack than those of Tony Allcock, and Ron is through to the semi-final.

The final in 1985 was between David Bryant, who had won all his previous games, and Cecil Bransky, the South African from Israel. In the final ends, which were televised, it was interesting to see that it was really a matter of drawing to the jack just as it would have been in a club roll-up. Advanced tactics did not seem to come into the battle. Certainly the length of the jack was amended from time to time but little else was evident, at least not to me.

David Bryant attempted a firing shot on one occasion but missed the jack. If David, this champion of champions who started playing the game at the age of eight, can miss firing shots what hope do we have of succeeding? Well, it can be a very useful ploy – Cecil Bransky saved two ends with such forceful shots. The various books on advanced bowling all cite a number of international matches where the game was won by good and almost constant firing or drive shots. Still, I am quite sure the beginner should forget all thoughts of trying such drastic action! An accurate firing shot is extremely difficult to achieve and you gain nothing if you miss. Yet a draw to the jack is reasonably safe and it is a shot you have been practising ever since you set foot on the green. It is in most cases better to save one or two by drawing reasonably near to the jack than to waste your bowl on a wide drive. Remember also that a forceful drive will almost certainly upset the smooth delivery of your next bowl.

The new bowler may be heartened to know that these two great international champions in this final did not always place their woods in a close head around the jack. Sometimes the woods were quite widely spread and now and again even they delivered a short wood.

On the 16th end Cecil Bransky cast the jack into the ditch – I had thought I was the only one to perform such tricks! The jack was then correctly returned for David Bryant to cast and to reposition the mat if he so desired. David did not wish to repeat his opponent's error on this now dry and rather fast central section of the rink, so he used the useful ploy of aiming the jack slightly across the rink and not, as is normal, straight down the centre. This angled shot gave him more length to play with and also the jack is, near the end of its run, slowed by the more upstanding and untrampled grass away from the central area. The jack is then centred in the normal way. You must, of course, ensure that the jack is not so far angled as to leave the side boundary of the rink!

David Bryant finally won that match 21-12 after 20 ends. He won £5,500 plus possession for the year of the imposing Gateway Masters trophy. It was David's fifth win in the eight years since this Worthing tournament was instituted in 1978 to mark the 75th anniversary of the foundation of the EBA. Why is he so consistently good? No doubt he would put it down to practice and more practice, with a good measure of dedication to his game plus concentration. You can see that concentration oozing out of him as he stands, or rather crouches, on the mat. He is never hurried and has one object in mind: to deliver that bowl to rest exactly where he wants it.

We are fortunate in that David Bryant has written several excellent books in which he has endeavoured to pass on his knowledge and skills, but really the all-important practice and concentration is up to you – it cannot be learned from a book.

When the VTS Superbowl indoor match at Manchester, sponsored by Liverpool

Victoria Insurance, was first shown earlier in the year I had never seen the inside of an indoor rink. As it happens the rink I saw there bears little relation to the normal club arrangement, for this single rink with its tiered seating each side was, I believe, especially built for television coverage. Some rinks seen on television are portable and can be moved around the country – a great advantage. Nevertheless, the basic arrangement and the playing conditions are much the same as those I later encountered when I visited my local indoor club.

The non-bowling viewer can, however, gain an incorrect impression of the game from these televised matches, which are often specially tailored to give the sponsors their just publicity. You will see only singles matches on these special rinks: the normal uninterrupted progress of the scoring is divided up into sets (in some cases to give the television company opportunities to work in the advertisements). In normal club sessions you are more likely to find orthodox triples or fours games in progress with conventional progressive scoring. Having established these basic differences between television and club play, we can sit back and enjoy the sport and the opportunity of watching masters pitting their skills against each other.

I have noted how frequently they walk up to the head to examine the exact position of the woods. It is at first surprising how little one can see while standing on the mat placed some 25 yards from the jack. A bowl may seem to rest two inches from the jack whereas it is actually two or three feet away. The marker can give an approximate idea if requested to do so but he obviously cannot indicate the lie of each bowl or the relationship of one to the other. Hence the need in championship games for a personal inspection – the stakes are very high! However, if in a friendly club game you were to walk up to the head before every delivery you would be well and truly frowned upon for wasting time.

One aspect of this televised indoor game is that the shirts of the two players are coloured to match the identifying stickers on the bowls. Willie Wood in the VTS Superbowl is playing with red-marked bowls and wearing a red shirt, and his score will also be shown on the board against a red background so that the bowls, bowler and his score can be instantly linked.

The advent of television has brought into fashion the helpful practice of the marker holding up coloured indicator sticks to show which player he thinks is holding shot and the number of such scoring bowls. In this case Willie Wood has three scoring woods so three red indicators are held up. While the game is in progress these indications help the players as well as the perhaps unsighted audience. At the completion of the end the indicators also help the scorer.

In the CIS Insurance UK Bowls Indoor Singles Championship, 1985, held at the Guild Hall, Preston, it is interesting to see that these would-be singles champions find it, like me, easier to judge the green than to obtain the correct weight or length. Their woods, as seen by the camera situated behind the jack, very often lie in an almost straight line in front of and behind the jack, a fore and aft distance of perhaps two or three feet but almost dead accurate for line. The correct green is easier to gauge and to maintain than the length. The CIS event was, incidentally, played on the same portable rink as the Liverpool Victoria Insurance tournament, but with a different underlay under the same carpet.

As I have previously noted, these high-powered games between master bowlers really depend on the accuracy of the draw to the jack. This is the basis of any game and until you can achieve it with some consistency the study of advanced tactics is largely a waste of time and energy. Learn to walk or draw before you try to run or fire. Indeed, in this

Take heart, even the masters bowl short (or perhaps the jack has been knocked back). They can even deliver a jack into the ditch or get the bias wrong, so there's hope for us all!

evenly matched semi-final between John Watson and John Bell, neither attempted a single firing shot. It was a tantalising duel of drawing with no fancy shots and no playing to the gallery.

If you are concerned with tactics or if you enjoy post mortems, the video records will give you great scope for serious study. The televised presentation gives you a close-up view of the head after nearly every delivery. You can then study the position of the various bowls and their relation to the jack and to each other. After a few shots you can freeze this view of the head and reconstruct the position of play on your own carpet in front of the television set. Remember that you should not leave the tape recording frozen or static at one point for longer than a few moments otherwise you may damage the tape – check the instructions issued with your video recorder if you are in any doubt.

You can realistically reconstruct the head as it appears at any given time in the progress of the game by having available two sets of bowls and a jack. I have found it very convenient to purchase a set of Henselite home carpet biased bowls which are in effect miniature woods of light weight. If you do not wish to purchase such a home game outfit you could bring into use eight red billiard balls and the white cue ball, but the full-sized or the miniature biased bowls will give you more fun and interest. You are now in a position to pit your wits against the masters!

For example, stop your recording about halfway through the end when the head contains say four woods around the jack. Now arrange your bowls in the same relative position. Look at the pattern from the delivery end as if your were standing on the mat. Where would you place your next shot and at what strength? Well, you can move your bowl into your chosen position or carry out a gentle trickle delivery. Do not use a strong shot indoors as the full-size bowls are tougher than your furniture or paint! If you do trickle to your chosen position the bias will have its effect in a realistic manner, but if you are playing with the billiard balls the result will of course not be the same as there is no bias.

It is most unlikely that your carpet will have exactly the same effect on your bowls as the surface used in the televised match but, nevertheless, you can experiment endlessly. Would a nice draw have won the day? Would a yard-on stronger delivery have turned defeat into victory? Might a firing shot have paid dividends? How many alternatives were open to each player? Did they in fact play the correct shot?

Re-start your recording, observe what the masters did and try to work out why they opted for that procedure. Add your extra bowls to bring your reconstruction up to date. The whole strategy has most probably changed. How would you tackle the new situation? How did the experts react? Yes, you can have great fun on a cold winter evening playing your own fireside version of the Gateway Masters!

The same type of tactical reconstruction has often been used by coaches and others giving group instruction. A blackboard type rink can be set up with mock bowls placed upon the upright background by means of magnetic strips. However, for the solo or pairs reconstruction in front of a television recording, real bowls or miniature versions of them will take some beating especially as wicks, knock-ons and other features of actual play come into the action.

Some very interesting information on the televising of various types of bowls tournaments is given in *The BBC Book of Bowls*.

The advent of television and in particular of the video recorder has enabled various teaching tapes to be prepared and sold internationally. One example is an Australian tape prepared by the Royal Victorian Bowls Association with the approval of the Australian Bowls Council, presented by Henselite and entitled *Bowling in the Groove*. It is concerned with the basic delivery and the aim is to instruct the viewer in a sound basic movement. Useful dos and don'ts are given and presented in a manner which the viewer will find easy to remember.

The film runs for 20 minutes, rather short perhaps, but much helpful advice is given. This video tape is concerned only with advice on achieving a good, sound delivery technique. No doubt in the future other, perhaps longer, video recordings will be prepared and marketed on other aspects of the game of bowls. I, for one, will be a buyer!

A British production filmed on my home Beach House Park greens at Worthing with Roy Downing and various specialists including David Bryant and Jimmy Davidson – the chief British National Coach – runs for approximately one hour but the advice given is not as concentrated as in *Bowling in the Groove*.

The film, *Bowls Masterclass,* is sponsored by Thomas Taylor (Bowls) Ltd, the makers of Lignoid Bowls. It is claimed that 'the presentation is designed to help you to make the very best of your game, and to increase your enjoyment whether you are an enthusiastic novice or an experienced player. Grips are shown in close-up detail. Stance, back-swing and follow-through are fully demonstrated and their effect on line and length discussed. Weight control and rink judgement are covered, and the champions reveal their own match play tactics with explanations of shot selection and strategies'. I was pleased to read that the contents also included a 'remedial clinic', pinpointing and correcting common faults, and 'purposeful practise', on-green practice exercises especially constructed to improve performance levels for different shots and competition play.

Alas I have to report that this video did not live up to my expectations! Certainly I found it very unhelpful to the novice: no terms used were explained and very little practical advice was given. This presentation is not my idea of a 'masterclass' as very little tuition is given. The shorter Australian video I found much more informative and helpful. While I think a good video can be of great benefit to new players, this one, I am sorry to report, leaves much to be desired.

With a book one can thumb through the pages before purchase and form some opinion as to its contents and the number of helpful illustrations. With a video one has to buy blind and hope for the best!

Another Australian video for the beginner, *In the Groove,* is packed with useful information presented in a very professional way. The main sections of this 35-minute film include The Selection of Bowls, Rolling the Jack, Gripping the Bowl, Aiming or Grass-Line, Control of Length and there is a good demonstration of the various basic shots. Sound advice is given on individual practice.

While some of the Australian aspects may seem strange to British players – the marked central line down the rink, the white mats and the metric measurements – the film is basically very good and highly instructive. It is a great improvement on the previous two which I have mentioned. It is presented by sponsors Mazda, with the help of the Australian Bowls Council and leading Australian bowlers, as is a related film angled at the more advanced player; *Top Draw.*

This advanced techniques tape runs for 38 minutes. I found it very helpful, much better than others I have seen and reviewed, although there is scope for better coverage of some aspects of the game. I think this presentation would be best regarded as a sequel to *In the Groove* rather than an aid to the advanced player. The emphasis is on the singles game, not on match play, and thus no advice is given on the different team positions. Both tapes are correctly very much concerned with accurate drawing to the jack and with the techniques and practice needed to achieve this aim consistently. These tapes should be available at specialist shops stocking bowling equipment.

Although as a beginner earnestly striving to improve his game I find these instructional videos helpful, I think it fair to state that in price they compare unfavourably with a good book or, for that matter, with a live coaching course.

Looking Ahead and General Advice

I have in this introductory book confined my attention to personal experiences during my first 12 months' play. The coverage has consequently been rather basic, being concerned with the simplest aspects of the game. I, and no doubt you, wish to advance further, to become a good rather than an average player. How does one accomplish this ideal?

The simple answer is the old one: practice, practice and still more practice! Although this cannot be the complete answer, I shall not forget the importance of practice on the green. I shall always remember how I marvelled at a tall, upright senior citizen I saw during my first year. There he was, delivering so smoothly bowl after bowl, each one nestling up closely to the jack. I could not understand the necessity for this person to waste his time and money on such daily personal practice. He had obviously long since achieved perfection. I was to learn later that this figure was Norman King, an Olympic Gold Medallist and a sportsman who had won every honour going. Yet here he was, in his early 70s, steadily delivering one excellent wood after another. I realise now that he reached such heights only because he had always been prepared to practise, to perfect his technique, to keep himself in trim and to concentrate on the task in hand – in short – to strive to play the game of bowls better than anyone else.

Norman King, David Bryant and others have reached the top. So can we – they were beginners once. In fact today the novice player has advantages not enjoyed by earlier bowlers. The facilities are more plentiful; many more greens are available and indoor rinks enable players to pursue their game throughout the winter. It is now an all-year sport. Far more coaching facilities exist and the tuition is of a higher standard. The television screen enables you to study video tapes in the comfort of your own home, and also to look in on top quality bowls tournaments and matches, observing the cream of world-class bowlers in action. Above all there is a superb array of books to study.

David Bryant and other world-famous bowlers offer their experiences and pass on advice and help to all able to afford the modest cost of their books or who live within reach of a Public Library.

Now is the time, after your first bowling season, to read a selection of these books or to consider a week's coaching. The bowler's reference books merit careful study. I was very surprised to find how few of such books include an index, an omission that can be turned to our advantage. In addition to marking the relevant passages, I decided to prepare my own index to each of the books I wished to read. The act of preparing an index necessitates reading each page with great care – a beneficial exercise in itself – and noting on separate small sheets of paper each name, subject, piece of advice or hint as it occurs, together with the relevant page or illustration number. When you have worked your way through the book, you can sort out your papers into alphabetical order and copy out the result into a simple index such as you will find at the end of this book. Some may consider this to be a tedious task, and it is, of course, time-consuming, but I have found it most helpful. I have discovered which books are the most informative or useful for my particular needs – some are obviously stronger on some aspects of the game than others.

As you seek further to advance your interest and knowledge of the game, I would suggest that you subscribe to one or both of the two bowls magazines published in England. These are *Bowls International* and *World Bowls*. You will find that these publications contain many interesting articles and reports. In addition the advertisements will spotlight many opportunities. Have you thought of a bowling holiday? A number of excellent hotels seem to cater for the bowler, some sporting their own indoor or outdoor greens or running their own courses. At least one organisation runs bowls holidays, some in Spain. Details are also given of all the tournaments, and there are so many. Why not visit some – perhaps not yet as a competitor – you can learn from the giants and at the same time relax in the fresh air and sunshine. At 'Sunny Worthing' I am able to watch the Gateway Masters games, with the top international players the tournament attracts. If you require a front row seat, though, you will need to get up rather early! The magazine advertisements also feature a large selection of bowling equipment, clothing and accessories.

Turning from the written word, you will need to put the expert's advice or suggestions into practice. You should try out any experiments, a change of grip or mode of delivery, at private practice sessions rather than at an important match! I am all for experimenting to find the system or technique most suited to you the individual, but do remember that the standard styles of delivery or grip as now widely taught have been evolved over many years. They are followed with great success by the leading international players. It will surely be better for the relatively new player to perfect the tried and trusted methods before endeavouring to introduce to the world a new technique.

I shall therefore spend considerable time in the following years endeavouring to perfect my standard delivery. The basic requirement is still, and always will be, the draw to the jack. Once your delivery is in the groove, meaning that it is uniformly correct and comes automatically without thought, then you can turn to perfect shots or consider advanced tactics. Can you nine times out of ten rest four consecutive bowls within 12 inches of the jack? Such consistency seems strangely elusive.

During practice sessions try drawing to different-length jacks. Obtain two, cast one little more than the minimum 25 yards, the other the maximum length. Now bowl two of your four bowls to each of these jacks. You should have a good line to both but how is your judgement of length and the speed of the green?

If you have been playing as lead, as is usual for the beginner, you must expect to remain in that position for at least another season. Perfect your vital premier part in the team. Do you enjoy your private tussle with your opposite number and do you usually hold the shot wood before the number two takes your place? Does the skip smile at you and offer congratulations? Keep at it, perfect that draw to the jack.

Try to spot your own weaknesses and then strive to correct them. Do you deliver the jack to your skip's feet? If not, spend a few short sessions casting the little white one up the rink to pre-chosen points. See if you can borrow half-a-dozen jacks for an hour.

They will save time and much walking. Be sure only to practise with regulations jacks, not golf-balls which are of a different size and weight and are therefore worse than useless for your purpose.

Can you draw to a very short jack? Many players cannot. Again this tactic needs practice. It should be far easier to bowl a short distance but it is surprisingly difficult. Many new bowlers forget that you need to take very nearly the same grass-line as you would for a long run. Often you will still rest the wood short of the jack because you have over-estimated its closeness to the mat. Practise drawing to the short jack, not only will it pay dividends in match play but it is less tiring than bowling long sessions at a full-length jack.

Experiment with different placings of the mat. If you have mastered a short jack with the mat some six or seven feet from the ditch move the mat a further seven or eight feet up the rink. Then replace the jack the same distance up from the mat as you previously chose. You should still be able to achieve pinpoint accuracy, but can you? Has the movement of the mat upset your calculations? Master this play, future rivals may well try you out!

Test yourself. Can you cast a straight jack? Or even bowl a wood on the line you have selected? On a quiet day seek permission to bowl down a dividing string, or ask the green-keeper if he would sub-divide a rink with string for a practice session. By placing the mat astride the string or to one side of it if you prefer, cast a jack up parallel with the string, say an inch to the side. See how difficult it is. Likewise with the bowl. Although the bias will come into play as the bowl loses speed, a well-delivered bowl should still run straight along the path of aim for many yards. The faster the delivery, the longer the straight run. If it does not start parallel to the string it is simply the swing of your arm that is incorrect, or perhaps your stance. You cannot expect to bowl well until you can achieve a truly straight swing. Practise until it comes naturally.

While still mastering the position of lead, try to study the duties of number two or even number three. If you understudy them you will be ready to step up in position, if the occasion arises. Don't on the other hand be in a hurry to be skip. We probably all have dreams of being a brilliant skip, but there is much more to this key position than you might think. You will have to master all shots and know when to use each. You will need a deep understanding of tactics and to be able to bring the best out of your team. It will help to be a student of human character and in particular of the personalities of the various players in your team. That's for starters! Wait a bit before you put yourself forward to skip.

As you improve and wish to progress further do seek to play in more matches. The stronger the opposition the better, as long as you keep your eyes open. Watch the more experienced players – learn from them. Why did they win, was it merely that they bowled with more precision or did other aspects of the game give them command? On the same tack put your name down for as many competitions as you can. Play against as large an assortment of players as possible. Win or lose, it will be valuable experience, especially if you seek to analyse why you lost and endeavour to rectify your deficiency. For good all-round experience, why not lend a hand in the running of your club? Try to give any new member a helping hand and certainly welcome him or her as you would wish to have been greeted yourself.

While manners may not exactly make the bowler, they certainly help to ensure that the game is even more enjoyable for all. They also show that you have been around a little and have been brought up as a good club player who always remembers that sportsmanship overrides gamesmanship. Early in this book I remarked on my pleasure

Left. *Good concentration. This lady's bowls seem to sit up on her rather flat palm and she tends to keep her arm rather bent, but we all have individual methods and mannerisms.*

Below. *The mat placed on the string so that you can practice bowling straight down the line and test firing shots.*

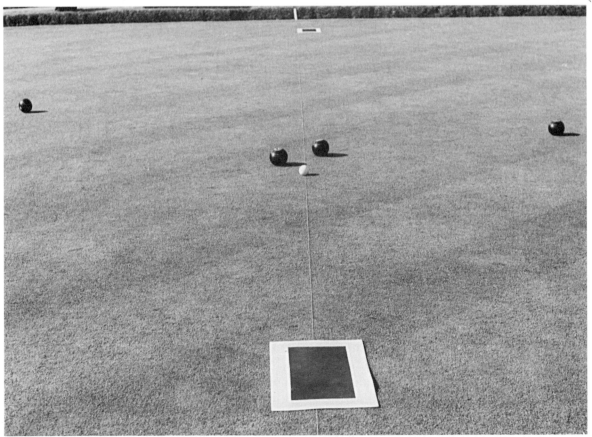

as I first stepped down on to a bowling green to be warmly greeted and introduced to all the team members (my own and the opposing team alike), who shook my hand and wished me good luck. The skip also invariably wishes everybody an enjoyable game. At the end of the competition too we all shake hands and offer congratulations or condolences. It is a gentlemanly game and in many more ways than this standard friendly introduction.

As lead, I make a point of speaking to my opposite number who, in my case, has always been much more experienced than I and senior in every other way. There is, of course, a great and important difference between speaking to him and being over-friendly by keeping up a never-ending conversation which distracts him while play is in progress. I certainly would not offer him advice on his bowling or on the tactics to be followed and would not expect this of him. I would, however, be inclined to pick up the mat and the jack and give these to him if his side had won the toss or the previous end. This is a generally accepted courtesy.

Assume for a moment that he has just bowled his wood and stepped forward off the mat. I would not make undue haste to take up my own position on the mat. He has possession of the rink up to the moment his bowl comes to rest. The few seconds this takes always seems too long, but take your time, relax and follow his bowl down the green with your eye and mind so that you can correct any error he has made in line or length. It is not only courtesy to wait your turn before taking your stance on the mat, it is also in your interests.

When you have taken your own turn, there are points to watch regarding both the governing Laws and etiquette, whatever you do after your delivery. You too have possession of the mat or the rink only until such a time as your bowl comes to rest. You must therefore be off the mat at that point and standing at least a yard behind the back edge. You should not be stranded halfway up the rink nor still standing over to one side. Both these clear faults are most distracting for the next player. He, if he is wise, should not endeavour to start his preparation for the delivery until you and everyone else are behind him, out of sight.

Although I write of sight it is equally important also to be out of sound! Do not chatter as a player is trying to settle down before his delivery. His mind must be free to concentrate on the job in hand. Remember also that, having delivered your own bowl, you are not then entitled to ask questions of the skip. He will probably make silent standard indications as to its distance from the jack, but any verbal questions must wait until you are once again in possession of the rink. Your bowl has stopped, and so must you!

If you should err on any of these points, do have the grace to apologise, so showing that you are aware of your lapse, and ensure that you don't repeat the offence. It may seem strange to some who have experience of other sports that there is no penalty for most infringements of rules or etiquette in the game of bowls. This most definitely does not mean that you can glibly override all conventions. Rather you are on your honour to obey rules and traditions.

Just as I have handed the mat and the jack to my opposite number so, when we come to walk down to the head, the leading number three or the lead will place his skip's wood ready for him on the mat. This third player will also probably hang back to consult with the skip as the players change ends. The skip may briefly explain his plan so that correct directions or advice can be given to him after the first bowl has joined the head. The third player may in turn offer advice or make useful comment on the running of the green. Once the players, less the skip, have reached the head they must quickly settle down behind it. Strictly, this means behind the most backward of the woods but in practice a certain amount of latitude is given (or taken) when there are one or two woods very much to the rear of the main pack.

Points to remember are that you must keep still. Don't walk around, don't point and don't do anything to distract. If you are standing in front of a few stray back bowls, remember that they are there and do not kick or displace them in any way. They may yet have a very important part to play in the result of that end. Be ready to jump or step out of the way if a long bowl comes speeding down. Be ready for ricochets or for a hit jack to move. Do not impede. You should also be on the look-out to catch a long wood just as it topples over into the ditch as a dead bowl. This should now be placed out of the way on top of the bank. It may be as well to confine such action to dead woods belonging to your own side to avoid any possibility of a dispute about whether the bowl was dead or not. Likewise, the collection of a dead wood that has come to rest beyond the side boundaries should be left to the side involved.

In collecting woods from the ditch bear very firmly in mind that a bowl which has touched the jack on its initial delivery is still live (provided that it has been correctly marked as a toucher) and must not on any account be moved. Remember also not to collect woods at the conclusion of the end until the score has been agreed by the number three of each side. In my first match, I witnessed a visiting player kick the bowls to the rear so displacing a disputed shot that was to have been measured. His side obviously had to concede the shot which could well have been a match-winner.

Practice targets; tennis balls with meat skewers through them, which can be placed on the rink or bank as points of aim.

There is provision in the rules for placing dead bowls on the bank in order to keep the ditch clear for the jack or for any live touchers. The bank should not be cluttered, however, with other equipment such as bags, unwanted jackets, hats and dusters. This is not the requirement of an overzealous green-keeper. Such regulations are necessary so that such objects are not used as aiming-points by players who – perish the thought! – might even have specially placed their yellow duster on the bank for that very purpose. Nevertheless one canny member of a club enjoys moving such bank litter around so as to foil any such attempt to gain an unfair advantage.

If for any reason you have occasion to send a bowl back up the rink when there are people at the receiving end, do remember to shout or otherwise give warning. A bowl travels silently and a blow on the shin can at best be extremely painful. Writing of returning bowls reminds me of the sound advice given to me by Norman King: always use a proper delivery action, never just pick up a wood and send it up the rink. You have spent months or years learning to make a correct smooth delivery in the groove, do not undo all this training by a thoughtless, undisciplined throw.

At the conclusion of the match (or even a roll-up) do not neglect to shake hands with all the other players, thanking them for an enjoyable game. Pleasant customs will probably extend to inviting your opposite number, or the visiting team, to have a drink at the bar – to play the '22nd end' – or to adjourn for tea if an afternoon match is being played. In this way the courtesies and friendliness of the green are further extended and friendships can be made to be renewed at the next meeting.

Make an effort to attend your club's AGM. By all means make constructive comments if invited to do so, for the officers should welcome interest and the opportunity to explain their actions or their apparent lack of action. If you are dissatisfied with the way in which the club is being run, be prepared to help put things right and to serve as an officer yourself if you are nominated. Be prepared to put in, not only to take out. Your enjoyment will be all the richer.

Bowling Equipment and Clothing

You can of course enjoy basic, casual games of bowls without the need to purchase any equipment. You can obtain the gear from green-keepers at most municipal parks which boast bowling greens. However, as you progress and perhaps join a club, you will need to own at least the basic equipment, such as your own special bowling shoes and your own bowls. After that, it is largely a question of the depth of your pocket and how seriously you intend to take up the game.

For the purpose of this Chapter I went along to my own local specialist bowling equipment dealer, Roy Downing, and asked him to fit out my 16-year-old son Jonathan who, as yet, has no bowling clothes or equipment. Jonathan is admittedly going to be rather more lucky than most new players who may have to purchase, from a variety of sources, unmatched oddments of bowling accoutrement as the need arises or as funds become available.

Jonathan and I enjoyed the advantage of discussing the necessity of the various items and the pros and cons of the different available types or makes with one who is not only an experienced bowler and coach but also a specialist supplier. This is an important point for, while most towns boast several general sports shops, the range of bowling equipment may not be very large, nor the owner or his assistant particularly knowledgeable on the needs of the bowler.

You will find that different suppliers offer similar equipment at varying prices. Some retailers, too, will be pleased to offer a discount to local club members who, after all, are regular customers and will recommend their shop and stock to fellow members. You can certainly shop around with advantage, but possibly the best long-term investment will come from patronising a specialist dealer who carries a large varied stock and is in a position to give you, the novice, the best advice. It is not all that helpful to buy a £100 set of bowls for a discounted price if they are not right for you. It has been known for completely the wrong basic types of bowls to be supplied!

Jonathan had reached (or almost reached) his maximum size, so that the clothing and equipment now purchased may be expected to last him many years. It would be foolish to buy expensive items for a boy or girl of 13 or 14 as they would obviously soon grow out of them. It is also advisable not to go overboard as a youngster's current interest in the game of bowls may quite conceivably be replaced with other activities as he or she matures. Nevertheless, for the purposes of this book, let us take Roy Downing's professional advice.

We were first concerned with shoes for, without these special, flat-soled, heel-less shoes, a bowler will not be allowed on a green. In the British Isles men wear shoes with brown uppers as opposed to the smarter – to my mind – white shoes favoured in most other countries. However, ladies sometimes favour white bowling shoes and Roy certainly stocks such elegant footwear.

Men's shoes come in various grades and therefore price ranges: one can buy quite respectable brown bowling shoes for around £20. Remember that you will be wearing these shoes for quite long periods, hopefully on hot, sunny days when your feet may well swell, so make sure they are not too tight.

Roy agrees with me that once one has decided to take up bowls one should go for the best quality pair of shoes one can reasonably afford. In the more expensive class Roy stocks the internationally-famous Dawn De Luxe, as recommended by David Bryant and other leading players. These are available at under £40; ladies' versions are slightly cheaper, say five pounds less than the mens'. Do not make the error of turning up for an important match in brand new shoes before they have been worked in for a few weeks. You should keep the uppers waxed and in a presentable condition. It is surprising how scuffed neglected bowling shoes become. Remember these special shoes are for use on the grass or carpet, you should not drive to the match in them or even walk on roads or pavements.

If you do not wish to go to the expense of buying special bowling shoes, which are not suitable for everyday off-green use, then you can purchase slip-on rubber overshoes. These are still, however, over ten pounds, and I have never seen a club player with such makeshift gear, but, they are available for the novice.

Special, flat-soled bowler's shoes – a must for all players.

I notice that sandals have now been introduced for ladies. These may well be cool and comfortable in high summer but I'm not sure that the open-toe design is conducive to kicking in the bowls. Still, they seem to have received official approval and they are cheaper than the standard all-leather conventional shoe.

If you are at the moment just enjoying roll-ups, you will not require the white socks that will later be needed for club match play along with white trousers. If you play often, however, you will need to carry spare pairs. Foot comfort and foot hygiene are very important. The socks should certainly not be tight and wool will be more suitable for some people than non-absorbent man-made materials.

For normal recreational play you will only need grey trousers of normal everyday type. They should be relatively loose fitting as one has frequently to stoop to pick up bowls and so forth. Light-weight material is preferable to a heavy winter cloth. You will need a stock of white shirts: one can be short-sleeved for summer days but, whatever the weather, your club will no doubt expect a tie to be worn and not an open neck. On the same gentlemanly tack, trouser-braces must not be visible, and white underwear is advisable. You should have a warm, white sweater or jacket available at all times.

Match play is of course continued in rain, necessitating white waterproof over-trousers, a matching jacket and a hat or cap. These come in various price ranges and in general it is preferable to buy the best. Some are only shower-proof, not watertight in a downpour or in persistent rain. One can really only leave you to choose your own waterproof to suit your financial standing. Do remember, however, that you will need to be able to play in these over-garments, so they need to be as comfortable as possible. Trouser-legs should be too long rather than too short, otherwise your shoes will fill with water.

It does not rain all the time, even in Great Britain, so you would be advised to have a light-weight cap or hat in your bag in case you have to play for several hours in the sun. These are quite inexpensive and can look very businesslike and smart.

Another useful little item is a metal enamelled name-badge to pin to your jacket or shirt. Some clubs order several at a time for their members and so enjoy a small discount.

If my wife Jean should decide to join Jonathan and me on the green she will require much the same type of regulation 'uniform' and equipment, although her bowls will be of the smallest permissible size to suit her small hands. As regards dress, ladies will need, of course, flat-soled heel-less brown shoes of the type sports dealers supply. You should wear a grey skirt, and this should be obtained from a specialist supplier as it needs to be rather longer than normal to permit a long forward delivery step. White jackets can also be obtained.

Once the lady player progresses to represent her club, white skirts will be required and some clubs may insist on regulation head-gear. Ladies' hats come in various styles and can be most attractive. It is possible that your club will have special colours for a shirt or a jacket.

Once you have climbed a little way up the bowling ladder you will probably need to purchase a smart club sports jacket, normally in navy-blue with the club badge or arms on the breast pocket. To this you may be able to add a multitude of medals, and awards – some veteran bowlers look more like Russian generals!

Let us now turn from dress to that most important item of a bowler's equipment – the bowls. These are the most expensive of our purchases for we need a set of four. For many, or most, new players I should perhaps advise the initial purchase of a second-hand set which can sometimes be had (via a club noticeboard, for example) for a pleasingly low price. If you later find that you have bought the wrong size, or the incorrect weight

Above. *Women bowlers correctly dressed for match play in their whites.*

Left. *Testing that a bowl is not too large a size. It should stay in your hand when reversed like this.*

or degree of bias, then they can be passed on again with little financial loss. However, for this exercise we will do the sensible thing and take good professional advice.

I must first point out that today all new bowls will be of press-moulded composition. They are supplied in black or in dark-brown tints known as 'mahogany' or 'walnut'. Most players follow Henry Ford's preference for black. Regarding finish, this can be either matt or gloss, that is manufactured with or without a polished surface.

Although the colours are limited, the variations in other characteristics are almost limitless. The basic international sizes range from 0 to 7, increasing upwards by $1/16$th of an inch for each size, measured around the circumference. The weight can also vary even within a size, so long as it does not exceed $3\frac{1}{2}$lb, while you can also purchase bowls with different built-in degrees of bias, of which bias 3 is the norm. You can also buy special bowls for indoor carpet play which take less green. Some players, particularly specialist leads, favour a rather smaller bias than the normal 3, but Roy and I agreed that all new players should start with the standard 3 biased bowl and learn to take a normal wide green-line, not to start with a below average, narrow line.

In choosing your bowl the essential point is to ensure that it is the correct size for your hand, that it is not too heavy and that it is comfortable. This is largely a personal decision and may be a matter of trial and error, although there are some generally accepted guidelines to bear in mind apart from the size-guides issued by some manufacturers.

Some stockists have a special gauge which indicates the correct size of bowl, but failing this the general preferred method is to span the would-be player's hands around the circumference of the bowl. The thumbs and middle fingers should just meet: the bowl is too large if the fingers will not touch. Having said this, some top players, coaches and authors now suggest that you should go up a size or even two above the ideal. Again it is a matter of choice or later experience, but remember that the weight also will increase with the size and that the whole object is comfort. You should not need to strain as any stress will affect your delivery. Your grip should not require tension of the muscles of the hand and fingers. However, to the beginner picking up a bowl for the first time, all may seem over-heavy.

Another method of testing the size and weight of the bowl is to hold it in your normal delivering grip and then reverse your hand so that the bowl is downwards. Now give the top of the hand a sharp knock. If the bowl stays in place it is a reasonable fit for your hand. One can also adopt a delivering stance and take a rather exaggerated back-swing. If the bowl drops out of your hand it is too large or too heavy for you and a smaller size should be tried.

Of course, the best test is to make real deliveries with a choice of differing bowls. You can to some degree accomplish this field-testing on a bowling green by borrowing different sets of bowls from fellow players. It is not always easy, however, to get six different players to loan you their woods at one time! And even if you do manage to find a set that feels right you will still have the problem of matching it with an available set in a shop. Here at Worthing Roy Downing has overcome this very real difficulty by setting up in his shop basement a small practice carpet rink with a sloping end so that the bowls are self-returning. Here one can test by delivering a dozen or more sets of bowls which are immediately available for purchase.

The price of a set of bowls can vary greatly from maker to maker and between the different models or types. Do discuss the pros and cons with practised players. Roy Downing stocks the very reasonably-priced Scottish-made Thomas Taylor Lignoid bowls which he recommends for the new player who may not wish to pay over about £60 for his first set. At an enhanced price there is a good range of the popular Australian

Henselite bowls. This company pioneered the modern composition bowl and their products are generally considered to be the ultimate. Of all the bowls used around the world, the Henselites are surely the most popular. I have a set of Henselite Supergrips, and I certainly have no complaint over the cost, nearly £100 in 1985, or their subsequent performance.

I now find that I could have spent more on a set of Henselite De Luxe Ezigrip which are slightly more expensive, but can be regarded as an investment and should outlast your golf clubs, your yacht and certainly your car!

There are several other makes, all with their devotees. You will find these stocked by various retailers or featured in advertisements in *Bowls International* or *World Bowls.* These popular leading makes or types include Drakelite, as recommended and used by David Bryant; Drakes Pride (manufactured in Scotland by Thomas Taylor Bowls); Almark (Made by the Henselite Company in Scotland); Crystalate, Greenmaster, Concorde, Tryolite and Vitalite.

Remember to specify clearly what basic type of bowl you are seeking: Outdoor Lawn bowls, Indoor bowls or Crown Green bowls. Most makers produce their bowls with or without turned-out grips. Again this is a matter of personal choice, but an indented grip pattern just inside the running surface seems to have advantages especially if you have hot, damp hands or if you are playing outdoors in wet conditions when the heavy bowls can certainly acquire eel-like characteristics. You can purchase various waxes which give an extra grip in wet conditions and polish your bowls. Henselite Grippo is one such preparation, a selection of which will be displayed in most specialist shops.

You will also need a good duster or special bowler's cloth to clean and dry your bowls before each delivery. This cloth is also the correct material for keeping your hands clean and dry. Be warned – a new household-type yellow duster can stain your whites badly in wet weather.

Whichever type of bowl you settle for, do treat it with respect and pride. Treat it as an infantryman does his rifle or you would your favourite pet. Keep it clean and well-polished, protect it and try to avoid any damage to it which may be caused in transit to and from games or throwing it into the ditch when not in play.

Having acquired a set of woods which will weigh in total over 12 pounds, you will almost certainly need a carrying bag for it is almost impossible to walk around carrying four loose bowls. These bags vary from the inexpensive and light string bags to very grand leather portmanteau-type containers. The more expensive ones seem to be very heavy and complicated, sometimes featuring separate sections for the bowls. Jonathan chose a roomy medium-priced bag with a single opening at the top. The bag should be sufficiently roomy to hold not only the four bowls and your shoes but also a change of clothing, weatherproof over-trousers and jacket, accessories and perhaps a flask. If you progress to playing in away matches you will need all your equipment neatly stowed for coach or car travel.

If you are quite certain you will never play away from your home green situated a few yards from the clubhouse, then you can dispense with the large expensive bag and rely on your locker and the string bag.

You can also obtain rather neat, small carrying bags which are designed to hold only two bowls. These are popular with players who mainly play in fours games and therefore need only two woods.

As far as accessories are concerned you will need firstly some type of measuring instrument if you are to play in serious games. The new player can get by without a measure as others will be able to lend him one if necessary, but you may not feel properly kitted-out until you have your own. Measures come in several basic types beginning with the inexpensive calipers (for use when the bowls are very near the jack) and the cord or string type. The latter is useful if a bowl or the jack is in the ditch and two objects to be measured are consequently not on a level plane. A rather more fancy measure is the pen measure or telescopic-rod device. This is slim and neat and will cost about four pounds. Often, however, these are not long enough. The most popular basic type seems to be the more expensive steel extending tape-measure which retracts into a slim box-like housing. Most of the more modern types have little feelers on the housing at a point level with the greatest circumference of the jack. The base of the container forms a reasonably steady base for the measure so that the jack is less likely to be displaced by fumbling hands.

Surprisingly no neat clean chalk-marker has been introduced for marking touchers, so one is obliged to use ordinary blackboard chalk. One's own scorecard-holder provides a nice touch – it is not a necessity but they cost only around two pounds. For club matches you will probably be provided with a stiff holder together with the scorecard.

If one was to purchase all this clothing and bowling equipment at one fell swoop the cost would be daunting, but this is not at all necessary. As you progress so you will need to own your own bowls and other personal requirements, but birthdays and Christmas help you to equip yourself or your family in a convenient way.

Points to Watch

I here list a few 'dos and don'ts', points to bear in mind if you are to bowl your best and do justice to yourself and to the rest of your team and club.

Some of these points may seem self-evident and obvious but they are based on observation of very common errors which are made even by very experienced players – not all but some.

Tension. Do keep cool, calm and collected at all times, it is only a game.

Never give in. The game is not won or lost until the last bowl has come to rest. I have seen the most surprising swings of fortune from one player to another. Keep at it, play to win even when you are ten or more points down.

Do not worry about a bad delivery. Forget it, and think only of the next bowl, but ensure that you avoid making the same mistake.

Do not worry if you are several shots or ends down. Concentrate only on your next delivery and future play.

Avoid firing shots when a draw would be simpler and more effective, if less spectacular!

Avoid altering the length of the jack or the position of the mat while you are winning ends. This tactic is correctly reserved for a losing position.

Do not be embarrassed by shortcomings.

Do not be afraid, in a singles match, to inspect the head. Or in other games to ask the skip for advice on the position of the jack or other bowls. Your picture from the mat can be restricted or distorted.

Watch your stance and make sure that one foot is *entirely* on or over the mat at the time the bowl is delivered. It is a basic Law and it should be the easiest to comply with.

See that your left (or right) foot steps forward in line with your grass-line during delivery, not straight down the rink. David Bryant advocates pointing your right big toe to the aiming-point.

Practise casting the jack to various predetermined lengths. Games can be won or lost on the delivery of a jack.

Take advantage of any opportunity to play in matches or to play with a better or more experienced player. You should learn much from observation, even if advice is not offered.

Do not let your mind wander. Concentrate on your own bowling; on your opponents' play; on the jack; on your green-line and aiming-point. It is surprisingly difficult to retain this concentration over a long game.

Practise and practise again but try to do this objectively. Practise on your weaknesses. Perfect your delivery until it becomes second nature, until you can bowl 'in the groove'.

Do not rush your practice, it can be exceedingly tiring. Having delivered one bowl, pause to allow time for a would-be opposing player to bowl, but use the time to work out any corrections necessary for your next delivery. Do not knock yourself out!

Bowl with a smile! Accept that your prize wood will probably be displaced by your opponents. Laugh and offer congratulations. Your turn will come to make a spectacular – or lucky – shot. Ensure that you are comfortable, that your clothing is not too tight. Avoid heavy meals or too much drink before a game or match. Be relaxed.

Be correctly dressed for the occasion and fully equipped. Have a pen or pencil available, a measure, chalk and, your cloth or duster to dry or polish your bowls.

Never ever rush your delivery. Take your time. If distracted, step off the mat and take a fresh stance. You are not in a race. On the other hand don't waste time unnecessarily.

Try your best to deliver your bowls well up to, or just past the jack. Do not block the approach with short woods.

Avoid taking too long a step forward with your left foot during the delivery. A natural step is all that is normally required, not a great stride.

Do not clear the bowls from the head before the score has been agreed by both sides.

Keep to your own task, do not duplicate or contradict the advice given by, for example, a number three.

Do not leave the mat on the grass when you stop playing, perhaps for a tea-break. The effect of the hot sun on the black rubber may well burn the grass and leave ugly patches on the playing surface. Rest the mat on top of the gathered bowls or leave it in the ditch.

In a doubles, triples or fours game, watch the skip. Follow his instructions – even if you are sure he is wrong! You are a member of a team, not an individual.

Keep still when not in possession, do not talk or otherwise distract a player.

Keep your bowls in a presentable, well-polished condition.

Know the Laws of the game but do not seek to shout your knowledge from the roof-tops.

Assist other players, especially the novice or the new club member and make them feel welcome.

Be ready always to take advice, to learn from the old hands. Offer thanks for such help, more may be forthcoming!

Be confident, play positively, make every bowl count and have a purpose.

Be a good club member. Support the elected officers, attend its functions. Play your part in running the club.

Enjoy your games – win or lose.

Appendix I
Laws of the Game

The following are the official Laws of Lawn Bowls, of Indoor Bowls and of the Short-Mat game in their entirety. These are, of necessity, couched in rather a heavy manner but nevertheless they should be read and re-read until they are thoroughly understood.

Over-abbreviated individual interpretations of the rules can be very misleading. I see, for example, that in the 1978 edition of the *Encyclopaedia Britannica*, no mention is made of centring the delivered jack and the text then states 'The Players then deliver their woods in turn by rolling them along the turf . . .'. The simple description 'deliver their woods in turn' is surely open to several incorrect interpretations.

Having a good working knowledge of the rules will give you added confidence when you are on the green. Please bear in mind that the Laws are amended from time to time. You should really equip yourself with up-to-date rule books which are quite inexpensive. These should be readily available from your club secretary or treasurer, from your local sports shop or direct from the various associations – such as the English Bowling Association – which governs the various versions of the one basic game of bowls.

Remember also that the rules are not the 'be all and end all' of the game; there are also many niceties that have grown up by tradition. Some may be unique to your club, others are internationally followed. These local rules or traditions facilitate the enjoyment of the game. They add to the basic regulations and do not supersede the official rules which all clubs and their members must follow.

LAWN BOWLS
LAWS OF THE GAME
(as revised in 1986)

The EBA handbook of the Laws commences with the following: 'It should be appreciated that no code of Laws governing a game has yet achieved such perfection as to cope with every situation. The code of Laws governing bowls is no exception. Unusual incidents not definitely provided for in the Laws frequently occur. It is well, therefore, to remember that the Laws have been framed in the belief that true sportsmanship will prevail: that in the absence of any express rule commonsense will find a way to complete a happy solution to a knotty problem.'

DEFINITIONS

1. (a) 'Controlling Body' means the body having immediate control of the conditions under which a match is played. The order shall be:
    (i) The International Bowling Board,
    (ii) The National Bowling Association,
    (iii) The State, Division, Local District or County Association,
    (iv) The Club on whose Green the Match is played.
    (b) 'Skip' means the Player, who, for the time being, is in charge of the head on behalf of the team.
    (c) 'Team' means either a four, triples or a pair.
    (d) 'Side' means any agreed number of Teams, whose combined scores determine the results of the match.
    (e) 'Four' means a team of four players whose positions in order of playing are named, Lead, Second, Third, Skip.
    (f) 'Bowl in Course' means a bowl from the time of its delivery until it comes to rest.
    (g) 'End' means the playing of the Jack and all the bowls of all the opponents in the same direction on a rink.
    (h) 'Head' means the Jack and such bowls as have come to rest within the boundary of the rink and are not dead.
    (i) 'Mat Line' means the edge of the Mat which is nearest to the front ditch. From the centre of the Mat Line all necessary measurements to Jack or bowls shall be taken.
    (j) 'Master Bowl' means a bowl which has been approved by the IBB as having the minimum bias required, as well as in all other respects complying with the Laws of the Game and is engraved with the words 'Master Bowl'.
    (i) A Standard Bowl of the same bias as the Master Bowl shall be kept in the custody of each National Association.
    (ii) A Standard Bowl shall be provided for the use of each official Licensed Tester.
    (k) 'Jack High' means that the nearest portion of the Bowl referred to is in line with and at the same time distance from the Mat Line as the nearest portion of the Jack.
    (l) 'Pace of Green' means the number of seconds taken by a bowl from the time of its delivery to the moment it comes to rest, approximately 30 yards from the Mat Line.
    (m) 'Displaced' as applied to a Jack or Bowl means 'disturbed' by any agency that is not sanctioned by these laws.
    (n) A 'set of bowls' means bowls all of which are of the same manufacture, and of the same size, weight, colour and serial number where applicable.

THE GREEN

2. The Green – Area and Surface:

The Green should form a square of not less than 40 yards and not more than 44 yards a side. It shall have a suitable playing surface which shall be level. It shall be provided with suitable boundaries in the form of a ditch and bank.

3. The Ditch

The Green shall be surrounded by a ditch which shall have a holding surface not injurious to bowls and be free from obstacles. The ditch shall be not less than 8 inches not more than 15 inches wide and it shall be not less than 2 inches not more than 8 inches below the level of the green.

4. Banks

The bank shall be not less than 9 inches above the level of the green, preferably upright, or alternatively at an angle of not more than 35 degrees from the perpendicular. The surface of the face of the bank shall be non-injurious to bowls. No steps likely to interfere with play shall be cut in the banks.

5. Division of the Green

The Green shall be divided into spaces called rinks, each not more than 19 feet, not less than 18 feet wide. They shall be numbered consecutively, the centre line of each rink being marked on the bank at each end by a wooden peg or other suitable device. The four corners of the rinks shall be marked by pegs made of wood, or other suitable material, painted white and fixed to the face of the bank and flush therewith or alternatively fixed on the Bank not more than four inches back from the face thereof. The corner pegs shall be connected by a green thread drawn tightly along the surface of the green, with sufficient loose thread to reach the corresponding pegs on the face or surface of the bank, in order to define the boundary of the rink.

White pegs or discs shall be fixed on the side banks to indicate a clear distance of 76 feet from the ditch on the line of play. Under no circumstances shall the boundary thread be lifted while the bowl is in motion. The boundary pegs of an outside rink shall be placed at least two feet from the side ditch.
(EBA Ruling: For 76 feet read 27 yards (24.69 metres).)

6. Permissible Variations of Laws 2 and 5

(a) National Associations may admit Greens in the form of a square not longer than 44 yards, nor shorter than 33 yards, or of a rectangle of which the longer side should not be more than 44 yards and the shorter side not less than 33 yards.

(b) For domestic play the Green may be divided into Rinks, not less than 14 feet not more than 19 feet wide, National Associations may dispense with the use of boundary threads.

MAT, JACK, BOWLS, FOOTWEAR

7. Mat

The Mat shall be of a definite size, namely 24 inches long and 14 inches wide.

8. Jack

The Jack shall be round and white, with a diameter of not less than $2^{15}/_{32}$nd inches, nor more than $2^{17}/_{32}$nd inches, and not less than 8 ounces, nor more than 10 ounces in weight.

9. Bowls

(a)   (i)   Bowls shall be made of wood, rubber or composition and shall be black or brown in colour and each bowl of the set shall bear the member's individual and distinguishing mark on each side. The provision relating to the distinguishing mark on each side of the bowl need not apply other than in International Matches, World Bowls Championships and Commonwealth Games.

Bowls made of wood (lignum vitae) shall have a maximum diameter of 5¼ins (133.35mm) and a minimum diameter of 4⅝ins (117mm) and the weight shall not exceed 3lb 8oz (1.59Kg). Loading of bowls made of wood is strictly prohibited.

(ii)   For all International and Commonwealth Games Matches a bowl made of rubber or composition shall have a maximum diameter of 5⅛ inches and a minimum diameter of 4⅝ins (117mm) and the weight shall not exceed 3lb 8oz.

Subject to bowls bearing a current stamp of the Board and/or a current stamp of a Member National Authority and/or the current stamp of the BIBC and provided they comply with the Board's Laws, they must be used in all matches controlled by the Board or by any Member National Authority.

Not withstanding the afore-going provisions, any Member National Authority may adopt a different scale of weights and sizes of bowls to be used in matches under its own control – such bowls may not be validly used in Inter-national Matches, World Cham-pionships, Commonwealth Games or other matches controlled by the Board if they differ from the Board's Laws, and unless stamped with a current stamp of the Board or any Member National Authority or the BIBC.

(iii) The controlling body may, at its discretion, supply and require players to temporarily affix an adhesive marking to their bowls in any competition game. Any tem-porary marking under this Law shall be regarded as part of the bowl for all purposes under these Laws.

(b) **Bias of Bowls**

The Master Bowl shall have a Bias approved by the International Bowling Board. A Bowl shall have a Bias not less than that of the Master Bowl, and shall bear the imprint of the Stamp of the Interntional Bowling Board, or that of its National Association. National Associa-tions may adopt a standard which exceeds the bias of the Master Bowl,. To ensure accuracy of bias and visibility of stamp, all bowls shall be re-tested and re-stamped at least once every ten years, or earlier if the date of the stamp is not clearly legible. (BIBC ruling for domestic play only. For ten years read fifteen years for all bowls stamped or restamped from 1.1.1977). (EBA Ruling: as from 1 January 1986 the re-stamping of composition bowls for competitive and domestic play in England is dispensed with. Bowls must, however, bear a legible stamp for 1985 or later, and can continue to be used without stamping until such time as the stamp becomes illegible.)

(c) **Objection to Bowls**

A challenge may be lodged by an opposing player and/or the official Umpire and/or the controlling body.

A challenge or any intimation thereof shall not be lodged with any opposing player during the progress of a Match.

A challenge may be lodged with the Umpire at any time during a Match, provided the Umpire is not a Player in that or any other match of the same competition.

If a challenge be lodged it shall be made not later than ten minutes after the com-pletion of the final end in which the Bowl was used.

Once a challenge is lodged with the Umpire, it cannot be withdrawn.

The challenge shall be based on the grounds that the bowl does not comply with one or more of the requirements set out in Law 9(a) and 9(b).

The Umpire shall request the user of the bowl to surrender it to him for for-warding to the Controlling body. If the owner of the challenged bowl refuses to surrender it to the Umpire, the Match shall thereupon be forfeited to the oppo-nent. The user or owner, or both, may be disqualified from playing in any match controlled or permitted by the controlling body, so long as the bowl remains un-tested by a licensed tester.

On receipt of the bowl, the Umpire shall take immediate steps to hand it to the Secretary of the controlling body, who shall arrange for a table test to be made as soon as practicable, and in the presence of a representative of the controlling body.

If a table test be not readily available, and any delay would unduly interfere with the progress of the competition, then, should an approved green testing device be available, it may be used to make an immediate test on the Green. If a green test be made it shall be done by, or in the presence of the Umpire, over a distance of not less than 25 yards. The comparison shall be between the challenged bowl and a standard bowl, or if it be not readily available then a recently stamped bowl, of similar size or nearly so, should be used.

The decision of the Umpire, as a result of the test, shall be final and binding for that match.

The result of the subsequent table test shall not invalidate the decision given by the Umpire on the green test.

If a challenged bowl, after an official test, be found to comply with all the requirements of Law 9(a) and (b), it shall be returned to the user of owner.

If the challenged bowl be found not to comply with Law 9(a) and (b), the match in which it was played shall be forfeited to the opponent.

If a bowl in the hands of a licensed tester has been declared as not complying with Law 9(a) and (b), by an official representative of the Controlling Body, then, with the consent of the owner, and at his expense, it shall be altered so as to comply before being returned to him.

If the owner refuses to consent, and demands the return of his bowl, any current official stamp appearing thereon shall be cancelled prior to its return.

(d) **Alteration to Bias**

A player shall not alter, or cause to be altered, other than by an official bowl tester, the bias of any bowl, bearing the imprint of the official stamp of the Board, under the penalty of suspension from playing for a period to be determined by the Council of the National Association, of which his club is a member. Such suspension shall be subject to confirmation by the Board, or a committee thereof appointed for that purpose, and shall be operative among all associations in membership with the Board.

10. Footwear

Players, Umpires and Markers shall wear white, brown or black smooth-soled heel-less footwear while playing on the green or acting as Umpires or Markers.
(EBA ruling only: Brown footwear only will be worn).

ARRANGING A GAME

11. General form and duration

A game of bowls shall be played on one rink or on several rinks. It shall consist of a specified number of shots or ends, or shall be played for any period of time as previously arranged.

The ends of the game shall be played alternatively in opposite directions excepting as provided in Laws 38, 42, 44, 46 and 47.

12. Selecting the rinks for play

When a match is to be played, the draw for the rinks to be played on shall be made by the skips or their representatives.

In a match for a trophy or where competing Skips have previously been drawn, the draw to decide the numbers of the rinks to be played on shall be made by the visiting Skips or their representatives.

No player in a competition or match shall play on the same rink on the day of such competition or match before play commences under penalty of disqualification.

This Law shall not apply in the case of open Tournaments.

13. Play arrangements

Games shall be organised in the following play arrangements:
    (a) As a single game.
    (b) As a team game.
    (c) As a side game.
    (d) As a series of single games, team games, or side games.
    (e) As a special tournament of games.

14. A single game shall be played on one rink of a Green as a single handed game by two contending players, each playing two, three or four bowls singly and alternately.

15. A pairs game by two contending teams of two players called Lead and Skip according to the order in which they play, and who at each end shall play four bowls alternately, the Leads first, then the Skips similarly.

(For other than International and Commonwealth Games, players in a pairs game may play two, three or four bowls each, as previously arranged by the controlling body).

16. A triples game by two contending teams of

three players, who shall play two or three bowls singly and in turn, the Leads playing first.

17. A fours game by two contending teams of four players, each member playing two bowls singly and in turn.

18. A side game shall be played by two contending sides, each composed of an equal number of teams players.

19. Games in series shall be arranged to be played on several and consecutive occasions as:
   (a) A series or sequence of games organised in the form of an eliminating competition, and arranged as singles, pairs, triples or fours.
   (b) A series or sequence of side matches organised in the form of a league competition, or an eliminating competition, or of inter-association matches.

20. A special tournament of games:

Single games and team games may also be arranged in group form as a special tournament of games in which the contestants play each other in turn, or they may play as paired off teams of players on one or several greens in accordance with a common time-table, success being adjudged by the number of games won, or by the highest net score in shots in accordance with the regulations governing the Tournament.

21. For International Matches, World Bowls Championships and Commonwealth Games, in matches where played,
   (i) Singles shall be 25 shots up (shots in excess of 25 shall not count), four bowls each player, played alternately;
   (EBA Ruling: Singles play under EBA jurisdiction shall be 21 shots up.)
   (ii) Pairs shall be 21 ends, four bowls each player, played alternately;
   (iii) Triples shall be 18 ends, three bowls each player, played alternately;
   (iv) Fours shall be 21 ends, two bowls each player, played alternately.
PROVIDED that pairs, triples and fours may be of a lesser number of ends, but in the case of pairs and fours there shall not be less than 18 ends and in the case of triples not less than 15 ends, subject in all cases to the express

approval of the Board as represented by its most senior officer present. If there be no officer of the Board present at the time, the decision shall rest with the 'Controlling Body' as defined in Law 1. Any decision to curtail the number of ends to be played shall be made before the commencement of any game, and such decision shall only be made on the grounds of climatic conditions, inclement weather or shortage of time to complete a programme.

22. Awards

Cancelled: see By-Laws after Rule 73 under heading 'Players' status and Involvements'.

STARTING THE GAME

23.(a) **Trial ends**
   Before start of play in any competition, match or game, or on the resumption of an unfinished competition, match or game on another day, not more than one trial end each way shall be played.

   (b) **Tossing for opening play**
   The captains in a side game or Skips in a team shall toss to decide which side or team shall play first, but in all singles games the opponents shall toss, the winner of the toss to have the option of decision. In the event of a tied (no score) or a dead end, the first to play in the tied end or dead end shall again play first.

   In all ends subsequent to the first the winner of the preceding scoring end shall play first.

24. Placing the Mat
   At the beginning of the first end the player to play first shall place the mat lengthwise on the centre line of the rink, the back edge of the mat to be four feet from the ditch. (Where ground sheets are in use, the mat at the first and every subsequent end, shall be placed at the back edge of the sheet – the mat's back edge being four feet from the ditch).

25. The Mat and its replacement
   After play has commenced in any end the mat shall not be moved from its first position.

If the mat be displaced during the progress of an end it shall be replaced as near as practicable in the same position.

If the mat be out of alignment with the centre line of the rink it may be straightened at any time during the end.

After the last bowl in each end has come to rest in play, or has sooner become dead, the mat shall be lifted and placed wholly beyond the face of the rear bank. Should the mat be picked up by a player before the end has been completed, the opposing player shall have the right of replacing the mat in its original position.

26. The Mat in subsequent ends

(a) In all subsequent ends the front edge of the mat shall be not less than six feet from the rear ditch and the front edge not less than 76 feet from the front ditch, and on the centre line of the rink of play. (EBA Ruling: For 76 feet read 27 yards (24.69 metres).)

(b) Should the Jack be improperly delivered under Law 30, the opposing player may then move the mat in the line of play, subject to Clause (a) above, and deliver the Jack, but shall not play first. Should the Jack be improperly delivered twice by each player in any end it shall not be delivered again in that end but shall be centred so that the front of the Jack is a distance of six feet (1.84 metres) from the opposite ditch, and the mat placed at the option of the first to play. If, after the Jack is set at regulation length from the ditch (6 feet, 1.84 metres) and both players have each improperly delivered the Jack twice, that end is then made dead, the winner of the preceding scoring end shall deliver the Jack when the end is played anew.

27. Stance on Mat

A player shall take his stance on the mat, and at the moment of delivering the Jack or his Bowl, shall have one foot remaining entirely within the confines of the Mat. The foot may be either in contact with, or over the mat. Failure to observe this law consitutes foot-faulting.

28. Foot-faulting

Should a player infringe the Law of foot-faulting the Umpire may after having given a warning, have the bowl stopped and declared dead. If the bowl has disturbed the head, the opponent shall have the option of either resetting the head, leaving the head as altered or declaring the end dead.

29. Delivering the Jack

The player to play first shall deliver the Jack. If the Jack in its original course comes to rest at a distance of less than 2 yards from the opposite ditch, it shall be moved out to a mark at that distance so that the front of the Jack is six feet (1.84 metres) from the front ditch. (EBA Ruling: If a mark has not been placed on the green the Jack shall be moved so that the front edge of the Jack is six feet (1.84 metres) from the front ditch and centred). If the Jack during its original course be obstructed or deflected by a neutral object or neutral person, or by a marker, opponent or member of the opposing team, it shall be redelivered by the same player, but if it be obstructed or deflected by a member of his own team, it shall be redelivered by the Lead of the opposing team, who shall be entitled to reset the mat.

30. Jack improperly delivered

Should the jack in any end be not delivered from a proper stance on the mat, or if it ends its original course in the ditch or outside the side boundary of the rink, or less than 70 feet in a straight line of play from the front edge of the mat, it shall be returned and the opposing player shall deliver the Jack but shall not play first. (EBA Ruling: For 70 feet read 25 yards (22.86 metres).)

The Jack shall be returned if it is improperly delivered, but the right of the player first delivering the Jack in that end, to play the first bowl of the end shall not be affected.

No player shall be permitted to challenge the legality of the original length of the Jack after each player in a singles game or leads in a team game have each bowled one bowl.

31. Variations to Laws 24, 26, 29 and 30

Notwithstanding anything contained in Laws 24, 26, 29 and 30, any National Authority may for domestic purposes, but not in any International Matches, World Bowls Championships or Commonwealth Games, vary any of the distances mentioned in these Laws.

MOVEMENT OF BOWLS

32. 'Live' Bowl

A Bowl, which in its original course on the Green, comes to rest within the boundaries of the rink, and not less than 15 yards from the front edge of the mat, shall be accounted as a 'Live' bowl and shall be in play.

33. 'Touchers'

A bowl which in its original course on the green, touches the Jack, even though such bowl passes into the ditch within the boundaries of the rink shall be counted as a 'live' bowl and shall be called a 'toucher'. If after having come to rest a bowl falls over and touches the Jack before the next succeeding bowl is delivered, or if in the case of the last bowl of an end it falls and touches the Jack within the period of half-minute invoked under Law 53, such bowl shall also be a 'toucher'. No bowl shall be accounted a 'toucher' by playing on to, or by coming into contact with the Jack while the Jack is in the ditch. If a 'toucher' in the ditch cannot be seen from the mat its position may be marked by a white or coloured peg about 2 inches broad placed upright on the top of the bank and immediately in line with the place where the 'toucher' rests.

34. Marking a 'Toucher'

A 'toucher' shall be clearly marked with a chalk mark by a member of the player's team. If, in the opinion of either Skip, or opponent in Singles, a 'toucher' or a wrongly chalked bowl comes to rest in such a position that the act of making a chalk mark, or of erasing it, is likely to move the bowl or to alter the head, the bowl shall not be marked or have its mark erased but shall be 'indicated' as a 'toucher' or 'non-toucher' as the case may be. If a bowl is not so marked or not so 'indicated' before the succeeding bowl comes to rest it ceases to be a 'toucher'. If both Skips or opponents agree that any subsequent movement of the bowl eliminates the necessity for continuation of the 'indicated' provision the bowl shall thereupon be marked or have the chalk mark erased as the case may be. Care should be taken to remove 'toucher' marks from all bowls before they are played, but should a player fail to do so, and should the bowl not become a 'toucher' in the end in play, the marks shall be removed by the opposing Skip or his deputy or marker immediately the bowl comes to rest unless the bowl is 'indicated' as a 'non-toucher' in special circumstances governed by earlier provisions of this Law.

35. Movement of 'Touchers'

A 'toucher' in play in the ditch may be moved by the impact of a Jack in play or of another 'toucher' in play, and also by the impact of a non-toucher which remains in play after the impact, and any movement of the 'toucher' by such incidents shall be valid. However, should the non-toucher enter the ditch at any time after the impact, it shall be dead, and the 'toucher' shall be deemed to have been displaced by a dead bowl and the provision of Law 38(e) shall apply.

36. Bowl Accounted 'Dead'

(a) Without limiting the application of any other of these Laws, a bowl shall be accounted dead if it:

　(i) not being a 'toucher', comes to rest in the ditch or rebounds on to the playing surface of the rink after contact with the bank or with the Jack or a 'toucher' in the ditch, or

　(ii) after completing its original course, or after being moved as a result of play, it comes to rest wholly outside the boundaries of the playing surface of the rink, or within 15 yards of the front of the mat, or

　(iii) in its original course, passes beyond a side boundary of the rink on a bias which would prevent its re-entering the rink. (A bowl is not rendered 'dead' by a player carrying it whilst inspecting the head).

(b) Skips, or opponents in Singles, shall agree on the question as to whether or not a bowl is 'dead', and having reached agreement, the question shall not later be subject to appeal to the Umpire. Any member of either team may request a decision from the Skips but no member shall remove any bowl prior to the agreement of the Skips. If Skips or opponents are unable to reach agreement as to whether or not a bowl is 'dead' the matter shall be referred to the Umpire.

37. Bowl Rebounding

Only 'touchers' rebounding from the face of the bank to the ditch or to the rink shall remain in play.

38. Bowl displacement

(a) Displacement by rebounding 'non-toucher' – a bowl displaced by a 'non-toucher' rebounding from the bank shall be restored as near as possible to its original position, by a member of the opposing team.

(b) Displacement by participating player – if a bowl, while in motion or at rest on the green or a 'toucher' in the ditch, be interfered with, or displaced by one of the players, the opposing skip shall have the option of:
  (i) restoring the bowl as near as possible to its original position;
  (ii) letting it remain where it rests;
  (iii) declaring the bowl 'dead';
  (iv) declaring the end dead.

(c) Displacement by a neutral object or neutral person (other than as provided in Clause (d) hereof):
  (i) of a bowl in its original course – if such a bowl be displaced within the boundaries of the rink of play without having disturbed the head, it shall be replayed. If it be displaced and it has disturbed the head, the skips, or the opponents in singles, shall reach agreement on the final position of the displaced bowl and on the replacement of the head, otherwise the end shall be dead. These provisions shall also apply to a bowl in its original course displaced outside the boundaries of the rink of play provided such a bowl was running on a bias which would have enabled it to re-enter the rink.
  (ii) of a bowl at rest, or in motion as a result of play after being at rest – if such a bowl be displaced, the skips, or opponents in singles, shall come to an agreement as to the position of the bowl and of the replacement of any part of the head disturbed by the displaced bowl, otherwise the end shall be dead.

(d) Displacement inadvertently produced – if a bowl be moved at the time of its being marked or measured it shall be restored to its former position by an opponent. If such displacement is caused by a Marker or an Umpire, the Marker or Umpire shall replace the bowl.

(e) Displacement by dead bowl – if a 'toucher' in the ditch be displaced by a dead bowl from the rink of play, it shall be restored to its original position by a player of the opposite team or by the marker.

39. 'Line Bowls'

A bowl shall not be accounted as outside any circle or line unless it be entirely clear of it. This shall be ascertained by looking perpendicularly down upon the bowl or by placing a square on the green.

MOVEMENT OF THE JACK

40. A 'Live' Jack in the Ditch

A Jack moved by a bowl in play into the front ditch within the boundaries of the rink shall be deemed to be 'live'. It may be moved by the impact of a 'toucher' in play and also by the impact of a 'non-toucher' which remains in play after the impact; any movement of the Jack by such incidents shall be valid. However, should the 'non-toucher' enter the ditch after impact, it shall be 'dead' and the Jack shall be deemed to have been 'displaced' by a 'dead' bowl and the provisions of Law 48 shall apply. If the Jack in the ditch cannot be seen from the mat its position shall be marked by a 'white' peg about 2 inches broad and not more than 4 inches in height, placed upright on top of the bank and immediately in line from the place where the Jack rests.

41. A Jack accounted 'dead'

Should the Jack be driven by a bowl in play and come to rest wholly beyond the boundary of the rink, i.e., over the bank, or over the side boundary, or into any opening or inequality of any kind in the bank, or rebound to a distance less than 61 feet in direct line from the centre of the front edge of the mat to the Jack in its rebounded position, it shall be accounted 'dead'.

(EBA Ruling: For 61 feet (18.59 metres) read 22 yards (20.12 metres).)

(National Associations have the option to vary the distance to which a Jack may rebound and still be playable for games other than International and Commonwealth Games.)

42. 'Dead' End

When the Jack is 'dead' the end shall be regarded as a 'dead' end and shall not be accounted as a played end even though all the bowls in that end have been played. All 'dead' ends shall be played anew in the same direction unless both Skips or opponents in Singles agree to play in the opposite direction. After a 'dead' end situation, the right to deliver the jack shall always return to the player who delivered the original jack.

43. Playing to a boundary Jack

The Jack, if driven to the side boundary of the rink and not wholly beyond its limits, may be played to on either hand and, if necessary, a bowl may pass outside the side limits of the rink. A bowl so played, which comes to rest within the boundaries of the rink, shall not be accounted 'dead'.

If the Jack be driven to the side boundary line and comes to rest partly within the limits of the rink, a bowl played outside the limits of the rink and coming to rest entirely outside the boundary line, even though it has made contact with the jack, shall be accounted 'dead' and shall be removed to the bank by a member of the player's team.

44. A Damaged Jack

In the event of a jack being damaged, the Umpire shall decide if another jack is necessary and, if so, the end shall be regarded as a 'dead' end and another jack shall be substituted and the end shall be replayed anew.

45. A rebounding Jack

If the jack is driven against the face of the bank and rebounds on to the rink, or after being played into the ditch, it be operated on by a 'toucher', so as to find its way on to the rink, it shall be played to in the same manner as if it had never left the rink.

46. Jack displacement

(a) If the jack be diverted from its course

while in motion on the green, or displaced while at rest on the green, or in the ditch, by any one of the players, the opposing skip shall have the jack restored to its former position, or allow it to remain where it rests and play the end to a finish, or declare the end 'dead'.

(b) Inadvertently produced. If the jack be moved at the time of measuring by a player it shall be restored to its former position by an opponent.

47. Jack displaced by non-player

(a) If the jack, whether in motion or at rest on the rink, or in the ditch, be displaced by a bowl from another rink, or by any object or by an individual not a member of the team, the two skips shall decide as to its original position, and if they are unable to agree, the end shall be declared 'dead'.

(b) If a jack be displaced by a marker or umpire it shall be restored by him to its original position of which he shall be the sole judge.

48. Jack displaced by 'non-toucher'

A jack displaced in the rink of play by a 'non-toucher' rebounding from the bank shall be restored, or as near as possible, to its original position by a player of the opposing team. Should a jack, however, after having been played into the ditch, be displaced by a 'dead bowl' it shall be restored to its marked position by a player of the opposing side or by the marker.

FOURS PLAY

The basis of the Game of Bowls is Fours Play

49. The rink and fours play

(a) Designation of players. A team shall consist of four players, named respectively, Lead, Second, Third and Skip, according to the order in which they play, each playing two bowls.

(b) Order of Play. The leads shall play their two bowls alternately, and so on, each pair of players in succession to the end. No one shall play until his opponent's bowl shall have come to rest. Except under circumstances provided for in Law 63, the order of play shall not be changed after the first end has been played, under penalty of disqualification, such penalty involving the forfeiture of the match or game to the opposing team.

50. Possession of the Rink

Possession of the rink shall belong to the team whose bowl is being played. The players in possession of the rink for the time being shall not be interfered with, annoyed, or have their attention distracted in any way by their opponents.

As soon as each bowl shall have come to rest, possession of the rink shall be transferred to the other team, time being allowed for marking a 'toucher'.

51. Position of Players

Players of each team not in the act of playing or controlling play, shall stand behind the jack and away from the head, or one yard behind the mat. As soon as the bowl is delivered, the skip or player directing, if in front of the jack, shall retire behind it.

52. Players and their duties

(a) The Skip shall have sole charge of his team, and his instructions shall be observed by his players.

With the opposing skip he shall decide all disputed points, and when both agree their decision shall be final.

If both skips cannot agree, the point in dispute shall be referred to, and considered by an Umpire, whose decision shall be final.

A skip may at any time delegate his powers and any of his duties to other members of his team provided that such delegation is notified to the opposing skip.

(b) The Third. The third player may have deputed to him the duty of measuring any and all disputed shots.

(c) The Second. The second player shall keep a record of all shots scored for and against his team and shall at all times retain possession of the score card whilst play is in progress. He shall see that the names of all players are entered on the score card; shall compare his record of the game with that of the opposing second player as each end is declared, and at the close of the game shall hand his score card to his skip.

(d) The Lead. The lead shall place the mat, and shall deliver the jack ensuring that the jack is properly centred before playing his first bowl.

(e) In addition to the duties specified in the preceding clauses, any player may undertake such duties as may be assigned to him by the skip in Clause 52(a) hereof.

RESULT OF END

53. 'The Shot'

A shot or shots shall be adjudged by the bowl or bowls nearer to the jack than any bowl played by the opposing player or players.

When the last bowl has come to rest, half a minute shall elapse, if either team desires, before the shots are counted.

Neither jack nor bowls shall be moved until each skip has agreed to the number of shots, except in circumstances where a bowl has to be moved to allow the measuring of another bowl.

54. Measuring conditions to be observed

No measuring shall be allowed until the end has been completed.

All measurements shall be made to the nearest point of each object. If a bowl requiring to be measured is resting on another bowl which prevents its measurement, the best available means shall be taken to secure its position, whereupon the other bowl shall be removed. The same course shall be followed where more than two bowls are involved, or where, in the course of measuring, a single bowl is in danger of falling or otherwise changing its position.

When it is necessary to measure to a bowl or jack in the ditch, and another bowl or jack on the green, the measurement shall be made with the ordinary flexible measure. Calipers may be used to determine the shot only when the bowls in question and the jack are on the same plane.

55. 'Tie' – No shot

When at the conclusion of play in any end the nearest bowl of each team is touching the jack, or is deemed to be equidistant from the jack, there shall be no score recorded. The end shall be declared 'drawn' and shall be counted a played end.

56. Nothing in these Laws shall be deemed to make it mandatory for the last player to play his last bowl in any end, but he shall declare to his opponent or opposing skip his intention to refrain from playing it before the commencement of determining the result of the end and this declaration shall be irrevocable.

GAME DECISIONS

57. Games played on one occasion

In the case of a single game or a team game or a side game played on one occasion, or at any stage of an eliminating competition, the victory decision shall be awarded to the player, team or side of players producing at the end of the game the higher total score of shots, or in the case of a 'game of winning ends', a majority of winning ends.

58. Tournament games and games in series

In the case of Tournament games or games in series, the victory decision shall be awarded to the player, team or side of players producing at the end of the tournament or series of contests, either the largest number of winning games or the highest net score of shots in accordance with the regulations governing the tournament or series of games.

Points may be used to indicate game successes.

Where points are equal, the aggregate shots scored against each team (or side) shall be divided into the aggregate shots it has scored. The team (or side) with the highest result shall be declared the winner.

59. Playing to a finish and possible drawn games

If in an eliminating competition, consisting of a stated or agreed upon number of ends, it be found, when all the ends have been played, that the scores are equal, an extra end or ends shall be played until a decision has been reached.

The captains or skips shall toss and the winner shall have the right to decide who shall play first. The extra end shall be played from where the previous end was completed, and the mat shall be placed in accordance with Law 24.

DEFAULTS OF PLAYERS IN FOURS PLAY

60. Absentee players in any team or side

(a) **In a single fours game,** for a trophy, prize or other competitive award, where a club is represented by only one four, each member of such four shall be a bona-fide member of the club. Unless all four players appear and are ready to play at the end of the maximum waiting period of 30 minutes, or should they introduce an ineligible player, then that team shall forfeit the match to the opposing team.

(b) **In a domestic fours game.** Where, in a domestic fours game, the number of players cannot be accommodated in full teams of four players, three players may play against three players, but shall suffer the deduction of one fourth of the total score of each team.

A smaller number of players than six shall be excluded from that game.

(c) **In a side game.** If within a period of 30 minutes from the time fixed for the game, a single player is absent from one or both teams in a side game, whether a friendly club match or a match for a trophy, prize or other award, the game shall proceed, but in the defaulting team, the number of bowls shall be made up by the lead and second players playing three bowls each, but one-fourth of the total shots scored by each 'four' playing three men shall be deducted from their score at the end of the game.

Fractions shall be taken into account.

(d) **In a side game.** Should such default take place where more fours than one are concerned, or where a four has been disqualified for some other infringement, and where the average score is to decide the contest, the scores of the non-defaulting fours only shall be counted, but such average shall, as a penalty in the case of the defaulting side, be arrived at by dividing the aggregate score of that side by the number of fours that should have been played and not as in the case of the other side, by the number actually engaged in the game.

61. Play irregularities

(a) **Playing out of turn.** When a player has played before his turn the opposing skip shall have the right to stop the bowl in its course and it shall be played in its proper turn, but in the event of the bowl so played having moved or displaced the jack or bowl, the opposing skip shall have the option of allowing the end to remain as it is after the bowl so played has come to rest, or having the end declared 'dead'.

(b) **Playing the wrong bowl.** A bowl played by mistake shall be replaced by the player's own bowl.

(c) **Changing bowls.** A player shall not be allowed to change his bowls during the course of a game, or in a resumed game, unless they be objected to, as provided in Law 9(c), or when a bowl has been so damaged in the course of play as, in the opinion of the Umpire, to render the bowl (or bowls) unfit for play.

(d) **Omitting to play.**

    (i) If the result of an end has been agreed upon, or the head has been touched in the agreed process of determining the result, then a player who forfeits or has omitted to play a bowl, shall forfeit the right to play it.

    (ii) A player who has neglected to play a bowl in the proper sequence shall forfeit the right to play such bowl, if a bowl has been played by each team before such mistake was discovered.

    (iii) If before the mistake be noticed, a bowl has been delivered in the reversed order and the head has not been disturbed, the opponent shall then play two successive bowls to restore the correct sequence.

    If the head has been disturbed Clause 61(a) shall apply.

62. Play Interruptions

(a) **Game Stoppages.** When a game of any kind is stopped, either by mutual arrangement or by the Umpire, after appeal to him on account of darkness or the conditions of the weather, or any other valid reason, it shall be resumed with the scores as they were when the game stopped. An end commenced, but not completed, shall be declared null.

(b) **Substitutes in a resumed game.** If in a resumed game any one of the four original players be not available, one substitute shall be permitted as stated in Law 63 below. Players, however, shall not be transferred from one team to another.

INFLUENCES AFFECTING PLAY

63. Leaving the Green

If during the course of a side fours, triples or pairs game a player has to leave the green owing to illness, or other reasonable cause, his place shall be filled by a substitute, if in the opinion of both skips (or failing agreement by them, then in the opinion of the Controlling Body) such substitution is necessary. Should the player affected be a skip, his duties and position in a fours game shall be assumed by the third player, and the substitute shall play either as a lead, second or third. In the case of triples the substitute may play either as lead or second but not as skip and in the case of pairs the substitute shall play as lead only. Such substitute shall be a member of the club to which the team belongs. In domestic play National Associations may decide the position of any substitute.

If during the course of a single-handed game, a player has to leave the green owing to illness, or reasonable cause, the provision of Law 62(a) shall be observed.

No player shall be allowed to delay the play by leaving the rink or team, unless with the consent of his opponent, and then only for a period not exceeding ten minutes.

Contravention of this Law shall entitle the opponent or opposing team to claim the game or match.

64. Objects on the Green

Under no circumstances, other than as provided in Law 33 and 40 shall any extraneous object to assist a player be placed on the green, or on the bank, or on the jack, or on a bowl or elsewhere.

65. Unforeseen incidents

If during the course of play, the position of the jack or bowls be disturbed by wind, storm, or by any neutral object the end shall be declared 'dead', unless the skips are agreed as to the replacement of jack or bowls.

DOMESTIC ARRANGEMENTS

66. In addition to any matters specifically mentioned in these Laws, National Associations may, in circumstances dictated by climate or other local conditions, make such other regulations as are deemed necessary and desirable, but such regulations must be submitted to the IBB for approval. For this purpose the Board shall appoint a Committee to be known as the 'Laws Committee' with powers to grant approval or otherwise to any proposal, such decision being valid until the proposal is submitted to the Board for a final decision.

67. Local Arrangements

Constituent clubs of National Associations shall also in making their domestic arrangements make such regulations as are deemed necessary to govern their club competitions, but such regulations shall comply with the Laws of the Game, and be approved by the Council of their National Association.

68. National Visiting Teams or Sides

No team or side of bowlers visiting overseas or the British Isles shall be recognised by the International Bowling Board unless it first be sanctioned and recommended by the National Association to which its members are affiliated.

69. Contracting out

No club or club management committee or any individual shall have the right or power to contract out of any of the Laws of the Game as laid down by the International Bowling Board.

REGULATING SINGLE-HANDED PAIRS AND TRIPLES GAMES

70. The foregoing laws, where applicable, shall also apply to single-handed, pairs and triples games.

SPECTATORS

71. Persons not engaged in the game shall be situated clear of and beyond the limits of the rink of play, and clear of verges. They shall preserve an attitude of strict neutrality, and neither by word nor act disturb or advise the players.

Betting or gambling in connection with any game or games shall not be permitted or engaged in within the grounds of any constituent club.

DUTIES OF MARKER

72.(a) The Marker shall control the game in accordance with the IBB Basic Laws. He shall, before play commences, examine all bowls for the imprint of the IBB Stamp, or that of its National Association, such imprint to be clearly visible, and shall ascertain by measurement the width of the rink of play (see note after Law 73).

(b) He shall centre the jack, and shall place a full length jack two yards from the ditch.

(c) He shall ensure that the jack is not less than 70 feet (21.35 metres) from the front edge of the mat, after it has been centred.
(EBA Ruling: for 70 feet (21.35 metres) read 25 yards (22.86 metres).)

(d) He shall stand at one side of the rink, and to the rear of the jack.

(e) He shall answer affirmatively or negatively a player's inquiry as to whether a bowl is jack high. If requested, he shall indicate the distance of any bowl from the jack, or from any other bowl, and also, if requested, indicate which bowl he thinks is shot and/or the relative position of any other bowl.

(f) Subject to contrary directions from either opponent under Law 34, he shall mark all touchers immediately they come to rest, and remove chalk marks from non-touchers. With the agreement of both opponents he shall remove all dead bowls from the green and the ditch. He shall mark the positions of the jack and touchers which are in the ditch. (See Laws 33 and 40).

(g) He shall not move, or cause to be moved, either jack or bowls until each player has agreed to the number of shots.

(h) He shall measure carefully all doubtful shots when requested by either player. If unable to come to a decision satisfactory to the players, he shall call in an Umpire. If an official Umpire has not been appointed, the marker shall select one. The decision of the Umpire shall be final.

(i) He shall enter the score at each end, and shall intimate to the players the state of the game. When the game is finished, he shall see that the score card, containing the names of the players, is signed by the players, and disposed of in accordance with the rules of the competition.

DUTIES OF UMPIRE

73. An Umpire shall be appointed by the Controlling Body of the Association, Club or Tournament Management Committee. His duties shall be as follows:

(a) He shall examine all bowls for the imprint of the IBB Stamp, or that of its National Association, and ascertain by measurement the width of the rinks of play.

(b) He shall measure any shot or shots in dispute, and for this purpose shall use a suitable measure. His decision shall be final.

(c) He shall decide all questions as to the distance of the mat from the ditch, and the jack from the mat.

(d) He shall decide as to whether or not jack and/or bowls are in play.

(e) He shall enforce the Laws of the Game.

(f) In World Bowls Championships and Commonwealth Games, the umpire's decision shall be final in respect of any breach of a Law, except that, upon questions relating to the meaning or interpretation of any Law, there shall be a right of appeal to the controlling body.

INTERNATIONAL BOWLING BOARD BY-LAWS PROFESSIONAL BOWLER

All players are eligible for selection for Commonwealth Games except those whose principal source of income is derived from playing the Game of Bowls.

STAMPING OF BOWLS

Each bowl complying with the requirements of Law 9 of the Board's Laws shall be stamped with the official stamp of the Board. The currency of the stamp shall be for a period of 15 years expiring on 31 December and the imprint on the bowl shall record the latest year in which such bowl may be validly used. (The 15 years referred to above is a BIBC decision for domestic play only.)

Any Member National Authority may make its own arrangements for the testing and stamping of bowls, and such bowls shall be valid for play in all matches controlled by that Authority. Provided that bowls comply with Law 9 of the Board's Laws as amended and bear a current stamp of the Board, and/or a current stamp of a Member National Authority, and/or the current stamp of the BIBC, such bowls may also be validly used in International Matches, World Championships, British Commonwealth Games, and other matches controlled by the Board.

Stamping of Bowls
Manufacturers will be entitled to use an oval IBB stamp, to facilitate the imprint between the inner and outer rings of bowls. Imprints on running surfaces should be avoided wherever possible.

Reproduced by kind permission of the International Bowling Board and English Bowling Association. Revised 1986.

INDOOR BOWLS
THE LAWS OF THE GAME

The following comprises the Laws of the Game Governing Indoor Bowls (third edition dated 1985), as published by the English Indoor Bowling Association.

Modestly priced copies, in a convenient pocketbook size, are available from indoor bowling clubs or direct from the Secretary of the English Indoor Bowling Association at 290A, Barking Road, London, E6 3BA. These rules may, of course, be amended from time to time.

Before quoting the formal rules (by kind permission of the Council of the EIBA) I would like to draw attention to part of the foreword:

'. . . Unusual incidents not definitely provided for in the Laws frequently occur. It is well, therefore, to remember that the Laws have been formed in the belief that true sportsmanship will prevail; that in the absence of any express rule common sense will find a way to complete a happy solution to a knotty problem . . .'.

DEFINITIONS

1. (a) **'Controlling Body'** means the body having immediate control of the conditions under which a match is played. The order shall be:

  (i) The British Isles Indoor Bowls Council,
  (ii) English Indoor Bowling Association,
  (iii) The County Association,
  (iv) The Club on whose Green the Match is played.

(b) **'Skip'** means the player who, for the time being, is in charge of the head on behalf of the team.

(c) **'Team'** means either a four, triple or a pair.

(d) **'Side'** Means any agreed number of Teams, whose combined scores determine the results of the match.

(e) **'Four'** means a team of four players whose positions in order of playing are named Lead, Second, Third, Skip.

(f) **'Bowl in Course'** means a bowl from the time of its delivery until it comes to rest.

(g) **'End'** means the playing of the Jack and all the bowls of all the opponents in the same direction on a rink.

(h) **'Head'** means the Jack and such bowls as have come to rest within the boundary of the rink and are not dead.

(i) **'Mat Line'** means the edge of the Mat which is nearest to the front ditch. From the centre of the Mat Line all necessary measurements to Jack or bowls shall be taken.

(j) **'Master Bowl'** means a bowl which has been approved by the International Bowling Board as having the minimum bias required, as well as in all other respects complying with the Laws of the Game and is engraved with the words **'Master Bowl'**.

  (i) A Standard Bowl of the same bias as the Master Bowl shall be kept in the custody of each National Association.

  (ii) A Standard Bowl shall be provided for the use of each official licensed Tester.

(k) **'Jack High'** means that the nearest portion of the bowl referred to is in line with and at the same distance from the Mat Line as the nearest portion of the Jack.

(l) **'Pace of Green'** means the number of seconds taken by a bowl from the time of delivery to the moment it comes to rest, approximately 30 yards (27.4 metres) from the Mat Line.

(m) **'Displaced'** as applied to the Jack or Bowl means 'disturbed' by any agency that is not sanctioned by these Laws.

(n) **'Ditch Holding Surface'** means some material other than the carpet to stop the jack or bowl from running along the ditch, e.g. pebbles, corks, Netlon, etc.

THE GREEN

2. The Green – Area and Surfaces

The Green shall form a rectangle or square of not less than 35 yards (32 metres) and not more than 44 yards (40 metres) long with a width of not less than 15 feet (4.57 metres). It shall have a suitable playing surface which shall be level. The ends shall be provided with suitable boundaries in the form of a ditch and bank.

3. The Ditch

The two end ditches shall have a holding surface not injurious to bowls and shall be free from obstacles. The ditch shall be not less than 8 inches (203 mm) nor more than 15 inches (381 mm) wide and it shall be not less than 2 inches (50.8 mm) nor more than 8 inches (203 mm) below the level of the green.

Ditches should also be supplied on the long side of the green, although this is not essential as the indoor greens are only used in one direction. If the land available is limited, the side boundaries may be supplied by wooden slats or boards or by a wall suitably cushioned so that bowls do not receive any damage on impact.

4. Banks

The banks shall be not less than 9 inches (228 mm) above the level of the green. No steps likely to interfere with play shall be cut in the banks. The surface of the face of the bank shall not be injurious to bowls.

5. Division of the Green

The green shall be divided into spaces called rinks, each not more than 19 feet (5.78 metres) nor less than 12 feet (3.6 metres) wide. They shall be numbered consecutively, and the numbers may be placed on the face of the bank, on top of the bank, or on the wall behind the bank on the centre line of the rink, which shall be marked on the face of the bank and flush therewith by a white slat made of wood or other suitable material not more than one inch wide, and the centre of the slat, which shall be marked by a thin black line, will mark the actual centre of the rink.

The four corners of the rink shall be marked by similar white slats fixed to the face of the bank and flush therewith, or alternatively fixed on the bank not more than 4 inches (101 mm) back from the face thereof.

Similar slats or discs shall be fixed to the side banks or wall to indicate a clear distance of 27 yards (24.7 metres) from the end ditch on the line of play.

Similar indicators may be fixed 6 feet (1.8 metres) on the side banks at each end to mark the position of the front end of the mat, and the position of the Jack at the opposite end.

An unobtrusive self adhesive marker in the form of a 'T' may be affixed to the carpet with the short leg of the 'T' parallel to 6 feet (1.82 metres) from the edge of the ditch.

6. No variations of the provisions of Laws 2 and 5 will be permitted unless (a) it can be established to the satisfaction of the National Executive that any such variation is essential to the efficient running of the club concerned or (b) such variation is permitted under the National Competition Rules.

MAT, JACK, BOWLS, FOOTWEAR

7. Mat

The mat shall be of a definite size, normally 24 inches (609 mm) long and 14 inches (355 mm) wide.

8. Jack

The Jack shall be round with a diameter of not less than $2^{15}/_{32}$ inches (63 mm), nor more than $2^{21}/_{32}$ inches (66.6 mm) and not less than 13½ ounces (382 gms) nor more than 16 ounces (453 gms) in weight, and of a colour as laid down by the BIIBC.

9. Bowls

(a)   (i) Bowls shall be made of wood, rubber or composition and shall be black or brown in colour, and each bowl of the set shall bear the member's individual and distinguishing mark on each side. The provision relating to the distinguishing mark on each side of the provision relating to the distinguishing mark on each side of the bowl need not apply other than in Championship and International Matches. Bowls made of wood (lignum vitae) shall have a maximum diameter of 5¼ inches (133.35 mm) and a minimum diameter of 4⅝ inches (117 mm) and the weight shall not exceed 3 lbs 8 oz, (1.58 kg).

(ii) For all Championships and International Matches a bowl made of rubber or composition shall have a maximum diameter of 5⅛ inches (130.2 mm) and a minimum diameter of 4⅝ inches (117 mm) and the weight shall not exceed 3 lbs 8 ozs (1.6 kg). Subject to bowls bearing a current official stamp. Loading of bowls is strictly prohibited.

(iii) The controlling body may, at its discretion, supply and require players to temporarily affix an adhesive marking to their bowls in any competition game. Any temporary marking under this Law shall be regarded as part of the bowl for all purposes under these Laws.

(b) **Bias of Bowls**

The Master Bowl shall have a bias approved by the International Bowling Board. A bowl shall have a bias not less than that of the Master Bowl, and shall bear the imprint of the Stamp of the International Bowling Board, or that of its National Association. National Associations may adopt a standard which exceeds the bias of the Master Bowl. To ensure accuracy of bias and visibility of stamp, all bowls shall be re-tested and re-stamped if the stamp is not clearly legible 1971 or later.

(c) **Objection to Bowls**

A challenge or any intimation thereof shall not be lodged with any opposing player during the progress of a Match. A challenge may be lodged with the Umpire at any time during a Match provided the Umpire is not a Player in that or any other match of the same competition.

If a challenge be lodged it shall be made not later than ten minutes after the completion of the final end in which the bowl was used.

Once a challenge is lodged with the Umpire, it cannot be withdrawn.

The challenger shall immediately lodge a fee of £1 with the Umpire. The challenge shall be based on the grounds that the bowl does not comply with one or more of the requirements set out in Law 9(a) and 9(b).

The Umpire shall request the user of the Bowl to surrender it to him for forwarding to the Controlling Body. If the owner of the challenged bowl refuses to surrender it to the Umpire, the match shall thereupon be forfeited to the opponent. The user or owner, or both, may be disqualified from playing in any match controlled or permitted by the controlling body, so long as the bowls remain untested by a licensed tester.

On receipt of the fee and the bowl the Umpire shall take immediate steps to hand them to the Secretary of the controlling body, who shall arrange for a table test to be made as soon as practicable, and in the presence of a representative of the controlling body.

If a table be not readily available, and any delay would unduly interfere with the progress of the competition, then, should an approved green testing device be available, it may be used to make an immediate test on the green. If a green test be made, it shall be done by, or in the presence of the Umpire, over a distance of not less than 25 yards (22.8 metres). The comparison shall be between the challenged bowl and a standard bowl, or if it be not readily obtainable, then a recently stamped bowl of similar size or nearly so, should be used.

The decision of the Umpire, as a result of the test, shall be final and binding for that match. The result of the subsequent table test shall not invalidate the decision given by the Umpire on the green test.

If a challenged bowl, after an official table test, be found to comply with all the requirements of Law 9(a) and 9(b), it shall be returned to the user or owner and the fee paid by the challenger shall be forfeited to the controlling body.

If the challenged bowl be found not to comply with Law 9(a) and (b), the match in which it was played shall be forfeited to the opponent, and the fee paid by the challenger shall be returned to him.

If the bowl in the hands of a licensed tester has been declared as not complying with Law 9(a) and 9(b), by an official representative of the controlling body, then, with the consent of the owner, and at his expense, it shall be altered so as to comply before being returned to him.

If the owner refuses his consent, and demands the return of his bowl, any current official stamp appearing thereon shall be cancelled prior to its return.

(d) **Alteration to Bias**

A player shall not alter, or cause to be altered, other than by an official bowl tester, the bias of any bowl, bearing the imprint of the official stamp of the Board, under penalty of suspension from playing for a period to be determined by the Council of the National Indoor Association of which his club is a member. Such suspension shall be subject to confirmation by the BIIBC or by a committee thereof appointed for that purpose, and shall be operative among all associations in membership with the BIIBC.

10. Footwear

Players, Umpires and Markers shall wear brown, smooth heel–less shoes while playing on the green or acting as Umpires or Markers.

ARRANGING A GAME

11. General Form and Duration

A game of bowls shall be played on one rink or on several rinks. It shall consist of a specific number of shots or ends, or shall be played for any period of time as previously arranged. The ends of the game shall be played alternately in opposite directions excepting as provided in Laws 38, 42, 44, 46 and 47.

12. Selecting the rinks for play – Umpire to witness

When a match is to be played, the draw for the rinks to be played on shall be made by the skips or their representatives. The actual rinks used will be decided by the club at which the game or games are played. In a match for a trophy or where competing skips have previously been drawn, the draw to decide the number of rinks to be played on shall be made by the visiting skips or their representatives. No player in a competition or match shall play on the same rink on the day of such competition or match before play commences under penalty of disqualification. This Law shall not apply in the case of open tournaments. For Association Competitions see Competition Rules.

13. Play arrangements

Games shall be organised in the following play arrangements:

(a) As a single game
(b) As a team game
(c) As a series of single games or team games
(d) As a special tournament of games.

14. A single game shall be played on one rink of a green as a single handed game by two contending players, each playing two, three or four bowls singly and alternately.

15. A pairs game by two contending teams of two players called lead and skip according to the order in which they play, and who at each end shall play four bowls alternately, the leads first, then the skips similarly.

(For other than International Matches, players in a pairs game may play two, three or fours bowls each, as previously arranged by the Controlling Body).

16. A triples game by two contending teams of three players, who shall play two or three bowls singly and in turn, the leads playing first.

17. A fours game by two contending teams of four players, each member playing two bowls singly and in turn.

18. A team game shall be played by two contending sides, each composed of an equal number of players.

19. Games in series shall be arranged to be played on several and consecutive occasions as:

(a) A series or sequence of games organised in the form of an eliminating competition and arranged as singles, pairs, triples or fours.

(b) A series or sequence of team matches organised in the form of a league competition, or an eliminating competition, or of inter-association matches.

20. A special tournament of games:

Single games and team games may also be arranged in group form as a special tournament of games in which the contestants play each other in turn, or they may play as paired-off sides of players on one or several greens in accordance with a common time-table, success being adjudged by the number of games won, or by the highest net score in accordance with the regulations governing the Tournament.

21. For Championships and International Matches where played:
(i) Singles shall be 21 shots up (shots in excess of 21 shall not count), four bowls each player, played alternately.
(ii) Pairs shall be 21 ends, four bowls each player, played alternately.
(iii) Triples shall be 18 ends, four bowls each player, played alternately.
(iv) Fours shall be 21 ends, two bowls each player, played alternately.

Provided that pairs, triples and fours may be of a lesser number of ends, but in the case of pairs and fours there shall not be less than 18 ends, but in the case of triples not less than 15 ends, subject in all cases to the express approval of the BIIBC as represented by its most senior officer present. If there be no officer of the BIIBC present at the time, the decision shall rest with the 'Controlling Body' as defined in Law 1. Any decision to curtail the number of ends to be played shall be made before the commencement of any game, and such decision shall only be due to, or on the grounds of shortage of time to complete a programme.

22. Awards

Cancelled; see By-Law 73 under heading 'Players' Status and Involvement'.

STARTING THE GAME

23. (a) **Trial ends**

Before start of play in any competition, match or game, or on the resumption of an unfinished competition, match or game on another day, not more than one trial end each way shall be played.

(b) **Tossing for opening play**

Two captains or skips in a team shall toss to decide which side shall play first, but in all single games the opponents shall toss, the winner of the toss to have the option of decision. In the event of a tied (no score) or a dead end, the first to play in the tied end or dead end shall again play first.

In all ends subsequent to the first the winner of the preceding scoring end shall play first.

24. Placing the Mat

At the beginning of the first end the player to play first shall place the mat lengthwise on the centre line of the rink, the front end of the mat to be six feet (1.82 metres) from the ditch.

25. The Mat and its replacement

After play has commenced in any end the mat shall not be moved from its first position excepting in the following circumstances:

(a) If the mat be displaced during the progress of an end, it shall be replaced as near as practicable in the same position.

(b) If the mat be out of alignment with the centre line of the rink it may be straightened at any time during the end.

(c) After the last bowl in each end has come to rest in play, or has sooner become dead, the mat shall be lifted and placed wholly beyond the face of the rear bank. Should the mat be picked up by a player before the end has been completed, the opposite player shall have the right of replacing the mat in its original position.

26. The Mat in subsequent ends

(a) In all subsequent ends the front edge of the mat shall be not less than six feet (1.82 metres) from the rear ditch and the front edge not less than 27 yards (24.7 metres) from the front ditch, and on the centre line of the rink of play.

(b) Should the Jack be improperly delivered under Law 30, the opposing player may then move the mat in the line of play, subject to Clause (a) of the Law, and deliver the Jack, but shall not play first. Should the Jack be improperly delivered twice by each player in any end it shall not be delivered again in that end but shall be centred in compliance with Law 29, and the mat placed at the option of the first to play.

27. Stance on Mat

A player shall take his stance on the mat, and at the moment of delivering the Jack or his Bowl, shall have one foot remaining entirely within the confines of the Mat. The foot may be either in contact with, or over the mat. Failure to observe this law constitutes foot-faulting.

28. Foot-faulting

Should a player infringe the Law of foot-faulting the Umpire may, after having given a warning, have the bowl stopped and declared dead. If the bowl has disturbed the head, the opponents shall have the option of either resetting the head, leaving the head as altered or declaring the end dead.

29. Delivering the Jack

The player to play first shall deliver the Jack.

If the Jack in its original course comes to rest at a distance of less than 2 yards (1.82 metres) from the opposite ditch, it shall be moved out to that distance and be centred, with the nearest portion of the Jack to the mat line being six feet (1.82 metres) from the edge of the opposite ditch. If the Jack during its original course be obstructed or deflected by a member of his own team, it shall be re-delivered by the Lead of the opposing team.

30. Jack improperly delivered

Should the Jack in any end be not delivered from a proper stance on the mat, or if it ends its original course in the ditch or outside the side boundary of the rink, or less than 25 yards (22.8 metres) in a straight line of play from the front edge of the mat, it shall be returned and the opposing player shall deliver the Jack but shall not play first.

The Jack shall be returned if it is improperly delivered, but the right of the player first delivering the Jack in that end to play the first bowl of the end shall not be affected. (See Law 26(b) above.)

No player shall be permitted to challenge the legality of the original length of the Jack after each player in a singles game, or the leads in a team game, have each bowled one bowl.

31. Variations to Laws 24, 26, 29 and 30

Notwithstanding anything contained in Laws 24, 26, 29 and 30, any National Authority may for domestic purposes, but not in any International Matches or Championships, vary any of the distances mentioned in these Laws.

MOVEMENT OF BOWLS

32. 'Live' Bowl

A Bowl, which in its original course on the Green, comes to rest within the boundaries of the rink, and not less than 15 yards (13.7 metres) from the front edge of the mat, shall be accounted as a 'live' bowl and shall be in play.

33. 'Touchers'

A bowl, which in its original course on the green touches the Jack, even though such bowl passes into the ditch within the boundaries of the rink shall be counted as a 'live' bowl and shall be called a 'toucher'. If after having come to rest a bowl falls over and touches the Jack before the next succeeding bowl is delivered, or if in the case of the last bowl of an end it falls and touches the Jack within the period of half-minute invoked under Law 53, such bowl shall also be a 'toucher'. No bowl shall be accounted a 'toucher' by playing onto, or by coming into contact with the Jack while the Jack is in the ditch. If a 'toucher' in the ditch cannot be seen from the mat its position may be marked by a coloured slat or marker about two inches (50.8 mm) broad placed on the top of, or on the face of the bank and immediately in line with the place where the 'toucher' rests.

34. Marking a 'Toucher'

A 'toucher' shall be clearly marked with a chalk mark by a member of the player's side. If in the opinion of either Skip, or opponent in singles, a 'toucher' or a wrongly chalked bowl comes to rest in such a position that the act of making a chalk mark, or of erasing it, is likely to move the bowl or to alter the head, the bowl shall not be marked or have its mark erased but shall be 'indicated' as a 'toucher' or 'non-toucher' as the case may be. If a bowl is not so marked or not so 'indicated' before the succeeding bowl comes to rest it ceases to be 'toucher'. If both Skips or opponents agree that any subsequent movement of the bowl eliminates the necessity for continuation of the 'indicated' provision the bowl shall thereupon be marked or have the chalk mark erased as the case may be. Care should be taken to remove 'toucher' marks from all bowls before they are played, but should a player fail to do so, and should the bowl not become a 'toucher' in the end in play, the marks shall be removed by the opposing Skip or his deputy or marker immediately the bowl comes to rest unless the bowl is 'indicated' as a 'non-toucher' in circumstances governed by earlier provisions of this Law.

35. Action of 'Touchers'

Movement of 'touchers' – a 'toucher' in play in the ditch may be moved by the impact of a jack in play or of another 'toucher' in play, and also by the impact of a non-toucher which remains in play after the impact, and any movement of the 'toucher' by such incidents shall be valid. However, should the 'non-toucher' enter the ditch at any time after the impact, it shall be dead, and the 'toucher' shall be deemed to have been displaced by a dead bowl, and the provision of Law 38(e) shall apply.

36. Bowl accounted 'Dead'

(a) Without limiting the application of any other of these Laws, a bowl shall be accounted dead if it:

    (i) not being a 'toucher', comes to rest in the ditch or rebounds on to the playing surface of the rink after contact with the bank or side wall or with a Jack or a 'toucher' in the ditch, or

    (ii) after completing its original course, or after being moved as a result of play, it comes to rest wholly outside the boundaries of the playing surface of the rink, or within 15 yards (13.7 metres) of the front of the mat, or

    (iii) in its original course, passes beyond a side boundary of the rink on a bias which would prevent its re-entering the rink. (A bowl is not rendered 'dead' by a player carrying it whilst inspecting the head).

(b) Skips, or opponents in singles, shall agree on the question as to whether or not a bowl is 'dead' (before the next bowl is delivered), and having reached agreement, the question shall not later be subject to appeal to the Umpire. Any member of either team may request a decision from the Skips but no member shall remove any bowl prior to the agreement of the Skips. If Skips or opponents are unable to reach agreement as to whether or not a bowl is 'dead' the matter shall be referred to the Umpire.

37. Bowl Rebounding

Only 'touchers' rebounding from the face of the bank to the ditch or to the rink shall remain in play.

38. Bowl Displacement

(a) Displacement by rebounding 'non-toucher' – bowl displaced by a 'non-toucher' rebounding from the bank shall be restored as near as possible to its original position, by a member of the opposing team.

(b) Displacement by participating player – if a bowl, while in motion or at rest on the green or a 'toucher' in the ditch, be interfered with, or displaced by one of the players, the opposing Skip shall have the option of:

    (i) restoring the bowl as near as possible to its original position;

    (ii) letting it remain where it rests;

    (iii) declaring the bowl 'dead';

    (iv) declaring the end dead.

(c) Displacement by a neutral object or neutral person (other than as provided in Clause (d) hereof):

    (i) of a bowl in its original course – if such a bowl be displaced within the boundaries of the rink of play without having disturbed the head, it shall be replayed.

    If it be displaced and it has disturbed the head, the skips, or the opponents in singles, shall reach agreement on the final position of the displaced bowl and on the replacement of the head, otherwise the end shall be 'dead'. These provisions shall also apply to a bowl in its original course displaced outside the boundaries of the rink of play provided such bowl was running on a bias which would have enabled it to re-enter the rink.

    (ii) of a bowl at rest, or in motion as a result of play after being at rest – if such a bowl be displaced, the skips, or opponents in singles, shall come to an agreement as to the position of the bowl and of the replacement of any part of the head disturbed by the displaced bowl, otherwise the end shall be 'dead'.

(d) Displacement inadvertently produced – if a bowl be moved at the time of its being marked or measured it shall be restored to its former position by an opponent. If such displacement is caused by a Marker or by an Umpire, the Marker or Umpire shall replace the bowl.

(e) Displacement by 'dead' bowl – if a 'toucher' in the ditch be displaced by a 'dead' bowl from the rink of play, it shall be restored to its original position by a player of the opposite side or by the marker.

(f) If a bowl in motion and on its original course collides with a similar bowl from another rink both bowls shall be returned to each player for re-delivery.

39. Line Bowls

A bowl shall not be accounted as outside any circle or line unless it be entirely clear of it. This shall be ascertained by looking perpendicularly down upon the bowl or by placing a square on the green, or by the use of a string or mirror or other optical device.

MOVEMENT OF THE JACK

40. A 'live' Jack in the Ditch

A Jack moved by a bowl in play into the front ditch within the boundaries of the rink shall be deemed to be 'live'. It may be moved by the impact of a 'toucher' in play and also by the impact of a 'non-toucher' which remains in play after the impact; any movement of the Jack by such incidents shall be valid. However, should the 'non-toucher' enter the ditch after impact, it shall be 'dead' and the Jack shall be deemed to have been 'displaced' by a 'dead' bowl and the provisions of Law 48 shall apply. If the Jack in the ditch cannot be seen from the mat its position shall be marked by a white slat or marker about 2 inches (50.8 mm) broad and not more than 4 inches (101.6 mm) in height, placed on top of, or on the face of the bank and immediately in line from the place where the Jack rests.

41. A Jack accounted 'dead'

Should the Jack be driven by a bowl in play and come to rest wholly beyond the boundary of the rink, i.e. over the bank, or over the side boundary, or into any opening or inequality of any kind in the bank, or rebound to a distance less than 22 yards (20.1 metres) in direct line from the centre of the front edge of the mat to the Jack in its rebounded position, it shall be accounted 'dead'.

42. 'Dead' End

When the Jack is 'dead' the end shall be regarded as a 'dead' end and shall not be accounted as a played end even though all the bowls in that end have been played. All 'dead' ends shall be played anew in the same direction unless both Skips or opponents in singles agree to play in the opposite direction.

43. Playing to a boundary Jack

The Jack, if driven to the side boundary of the rink and not wholly beyond its limits, may be played to on either hand and, if necessary, a bowl may pass outside the side limits of the rink. A bowl so played, which comes to rest within the boundaries of the rink, shall not be accounted 'dead'.

If the Jack be driven to the side boundary line and comes to rest partly within the limits of the rink, a bowl placed outside the limits of the rink and coming to rest entirely outside the boundary line, even though it has made contact with the Jack shall be accounted 'dead' and shall be removed to the bank by a member of the player's team.

44. A Damaged Jack

In the event of a Jack being damaged, the Umpire shall decide if another Jack is necessary and, if so, the end shall be regarded as a 'dead' end and another Jack shall be substituted and the end shall be replayed anew.

45. A rebounding Jack

If the Jack is driven against the face of the bank and rebounds on to the rink, or after being played into the ditch, it be operated on by a 'toucher', so as to find its way on to the rink, it shall be played to in the same manner as if it had never left the rink.

46. Jack displaced by player

(a) If the Jack be diverted from its course while in motion on the green, or displaced while at rest on the green, or in the ditch, by any one of the players, the opposing Skip shall have the Jack restored to its former position, or allow it to remain where it rests and play the end to a finish, or declare the end 'dead'.

(b) If the Jack be moved at the time of measure by a player it shall be restored to its former position by an opponent.

47. Jack displaced by non–player

(a) If the Jack, whether in position or at rest on the rink, or in the ditch, be displaced by a bowl from another rink, or by any object or by an individual not a member of the side, the two Skips shall decide as to its original position, and if they are unable to agree, the end shall be declared 'dead'.

(b) If a Jack be displaced by a Marker or Umpire in the process of measuring, it shall be restored by him to its original position of which he shall be the sole judge.

48. Jack displaced by 'non-toucher'

A Jack displaced in the rink of play by a 'dead' bowl rebounding from the bank shall be restored, or as near as possible, to its original position by a player of the opposing side. Should a Jack, however, after having been played into the ditch, be displaced by a 'non-toucher' it shall be restored to its marked position by a player of the opposing side or by the Marker.

FOURS PLAY

The basis of the Game of Bowls is Fours Play

49. The rink and fours play

(a) Designation of players. A team shall consist of four players, named respectively: Lead, Second, Third and Skip, according to the order in which they play, each playing two bowls.

(b) Order of Play. The leads shall play their two bowls alternately, and so on, each pair of players in succession to the end. No one shall play until his opponent's bowl shall have come to rest. Except under circumstances provided for in Law 63, the order of play shall not be changed after the first end has been played, under penalty of disqualification, such penalty involving the forfeiture of the match or game to the opposing side.

50. Possession of the Rink

Possession of the rink shall belong to the side whose bowl is being played. The players in possession of the rink for the time being shall not be interfered with, annoyed, or have their attention distracted in any way by their opponents.

As soon as each bowl shall have come to rest, possession of the rink shall be transferred to the other team, time being allowed for marking a 'toucher'.

51. Position of Players

Players of each side not in the act of playing or controlling play, shall stand behind the Jack and away from the head, or one yard (92 cm) behind the mat. As soon as the bowl is delivered, the Skip or player directing if in front of the Jack, shall retire behind it. In cases where there is no 'stand-off' room at the end of the rink, players shall stand well clear of the object bowl or Jack while a bowl is being delivered.

52. Players and their duties

(a) The Skip shall have sole charge of his side, and his instructions shall be observed by his players. With the opposing Skip he shall decide all disputed points, and when both agree their decision shall be final. If both Skips cannot agree, the point in dispute shall be referred to, and considered by, an Umpire whose decision shall be final.

A Skip may at any time delegate his powers and any of his duties to other members of his team provided that such delegation is notified to the opposing Skip.

(b) The Third. The third player may have deputed to him the duty of measuring any and all disputed shots.

(c) The Second. The second player shall keep a record of all shots scored for and against his side and shall at all times retain possession of the score card whilst play is in progress. He shall see that the names of all players are entered on the score card, shall compare his record of the game with that of the opposing second player as each end is declared, and at the close of the game shall hand his score card to his Skip.

(d) The Lead. The lead shall place the mat, and shall deliver the Jack, ensuring that the Jack is properly centred before playing his first bowl.

(e) In addition to the duties specified in the preceding clauses, any player may undertake such duties as may be assigned to him by the Skip in Clause 52 (a) hereof.

RESULT OF END

53. 'The Shot'

A shot or shots shall be adjudged by the bowl or bowls nearer to the Jack than any bowl played by the opposing player or players.

When the last bowl has come to rest, half a minute shall elapse, if either side desires, before the shots are counted.

Neither the Jack nor bowls shall be moved until each Skip has agreed to the number of shots, except in circumstances where a bowl has to be moved to allow the measuring of another bowl.

54. Measuring conditions to be observed

No measuring shall be allowed until the end has been completed.

All measurements shall be made to the nearest point of each object. If a bowl requiring to be measured is resting on another bowl which prevents its measurement, the best available means shall be taken to secure its position, whereupon the other bowl shall be removed. The same course shall be followed where more than two bowls are involved or where, in the course of measuring, a single bowl is in danger of falling or otherwise changing its position.

When it is necessary to measure to a bowl or Jack in the ditch, and another bowl or Jack on the green, the measurement shall be made with the ordinary flexible measure. Calipers may be used to determine the shot only when the bowls in question and the Jack are on the same plane.

55. 'Tie' – No shot

When at the conclusion of play in any end the nearest bowl of each side is touching the Jack, or is deemed to be equidistant from the Jack, there shall be no score recorded. The end shall be declared 'drawn' and shall be counted a played end.

56.

Nothing in these Laws shall be deemed to make it mandatory for the last player to play his last bowl in any end, but he shall declare to his opponent or opposing Skip his intention to refrain from playing it before the commencement of determining the result of the end and this declaration shall be irrevocable.

GAME DECISIONS

57. Games played on one occasion

In the case of a single game, team game or a side game played on one occasion, or at any stage of an eliminating competition, the victory decision shall be awarded to the player, side or team of players producing at the end of the game the higher total score of shots, or in the case of a 'game of winning ends', a majority of winning ends.

58. Tournament games and games in series

In the case of competitions on a time basis rules must be made to cover circumstances of each such competition.

In the case of Tournament games or games in series, the victory decision shall be awarded to the player, side or team of players producing at the end of the tournament or series of contests, either the largest number of winning games or the highest net score of shots in accordance with the regulations governing the tournament or series of games.

Points may be used to indicate game successes.

Where points are equal, the aggregate shots scored against each team (or side) shall be divided into the aggregate shots it has scored. The team (or side) with the highest result shall be declared the winner.

59. Playing to a finish and possible drawn games

If in an eliminating competition, consisting of a stated or agreed upon number of ends, it be found, when all the ends have been played, that the scores are equal, an extra end or ends shall be played until a decision has been reached.

The captains or skips shall toss and the winner shall have the right to decide who shall play first. The extra end shall be played from where the previous end was completed, and the mat shall be placed in accordance with Law 24.

In the case of more than one extra end being required then the captains or Skips shall again toss, and the winner shall have the right to decide who shall play first, in the case of an extra end being declared 'dead' then the provisions of Law 23(b) shall apply.

DEFAULTS OF PLAYERS IN FOURS PLAY

60. Absentee players in any side

(a) In a single fours game for a trophy, prize or other competitive award, where a club is represented by only one four, each member of such four shall be a current playing member of the club. The failure of all four players to appear and play after a maximum waiting period of 30 minutes from the time fixed for the start of the game, or the introduction of an ineligible player, shall cause the side to forfeit the match to the opposing side.

(b) In a domestic fours game. Where, in a domestic fours game the number of players cannot be accommodated in full sides of four players, three players may play against three players, but shall suffer the deduction of one fourth of the total score of each side.

A smaller number of players than six shall be excluded from that game.

(c) In a side game. If within a period of 30 minutes from the time fixed for the game, a single player is absent from one or both sides in a team game, whether a friendly club match or a match for a trophy, prize or other award, the number of bowls shall be made up by the lead and second players playing three bowls each, but one-fourth of the total shots scored by each 'four' playing three men shall be deducted from their score at the end of the game.

Fractions shall be taken into account.

(d) In a side game. Should such default take place where more fours than one are concerned, or where a four has been disqualified for some other infringement, and where the average score is to decide the contest, the scores of the non-defaulting fours only shall be counted, but such average shall, as a penalty in the case of the defaulting side, be arrived at by dividing the aggregate score of that side by the number of fours that should have been played and not as in the case of the other side, by the number actually engaged in the game.

61. Play irregularities

(a) Playing out of turn. When a player has played before his turn the opposing

Skip shall have the right to stop the bowl in its course and it shall be played in its proper turn, but in the event of the bowl so played having moved or displaced the Jack or bowl, the opposing Skip shall have the option of allowing the end to remain as it is after the bowl so played has come to rest, or having the end declared 'dead'.

(b) Playing the wrong bowl. A bowl played by mistake shall be replaced by the player's own bowl.

(c) Changing bowls. A player shall not be allowed to change his bowls during the course of a game, or in a resumed game, unless they be objected to, as provided in Law 9(c), or when a bowl has been so damaged in the course of play as, in the opinion of the Umpire, to render the bowl (or bowls) unfit for play.

(d) **Omitting to play.**

(i) If the result of an end has been agreed upon, or the head has been touched in the agreed process of determining the result, then a player who forfeits or has omitted to play a bowl, shall forfeit the right to play it.

(ii) A player who has neglected to play a bowl in the proper sequence shall forfeit the right to play such bowl, if a bowl has been played by each side before such mistake was discovered.

(iii) If before the mistake be noticed, a bowl has been delivered in the reversed order and the head has not been disturbed, the opponent shall then play two successive bowls to restore the correct sequence.

If the head has been disturbed Clause 61(a) shall apply.

62. Play Interruptions

(a) Game Stoppages. When a game of any kind is stopped, either by mutual arrangement or by the Umpire, after appeal to him for any valid reason, it shall be resumed with the scores as they were when the game stopped. An end commenced, but not completed, shall be declared null.

(b) Substitutes in a resumed game. If in a resumed game any one of the four original players be not available, one substitute shall be permitted as stated in Law 63 below. Players shall not, however, be transferred from one team to another.

INFLUENCES AFFECTING PLAY

63. Leaving the Green

If during the course of a fours, triples or pairs game a player has to leave the green owing to illness, or other reasonable cause, his place shall be filled by a substitute, if in the opinion of both Skips (or failing agreement by them then in the opinion of the Controlling Body) such substitution is necessary. Should the player affected be a Skip, his duties and position in a fours game shall be assumed by the third player, and the substitute shall play either as a lead, second or third. In the case of triples the substitute may play either as lead or second but not as Skip and in the case of pairs the substitute shall play as lead only. Such substitutes shall be a playing member of the club to which the side belongs. In domestic play National Associations may decide the position of any substitute.

If during the course of a single-handed game, a player has to leave the green owing to illness, or reasonable cause, the provision of Law 62(a) shall be observed.

No player shall be allowed to delay the play by leaving the rink or side, unless with the consent of his opponent, and then only for a period not exceeding ten minutes.

Contravention of this Law shall entitle the opponent or opposing side to claim the game or match.

64. Objects on the Green

Under no circumstances, other than as provided in Laws 5, 29, 33 and 40, shall any extraneous object to assist a player be placed on the green, or on the bank, or on the Jack, or on a bowl or elsewhere.

65. Unforeseen incidents

If during the course of play, the position of the Jack or bowls be disturbed by any neutral object the end shall be declared 'dead', unless the Skips are agreed as to the replacement of Jack or bowls.

DOMESTIC ARRANGEMENTS

66. In addition to any matters specifically mentioned in these Laws, a National Association may, in circumstances dictated by local conditions (and with the approval of the BIIBC where this is appropriate) make such other regulations as are deemed necessary and desirable. For this purpose the Association shall appoint a Committee to be known as the 'Laws Committee', with power to grant approval or otherwise to any proposal; such decision being valid until the proposal is submitted to the BIIBC for a final decision.

67. Local Arrangements

Affiliated or member clubs shall, in making their local arrangements, make such regulations as are deemed necessary to govern their club competitions; but such regulations shall be approved by the National Association and be displayed.

68. National Visiting Teams

No team of bowlers visiting overseas or the British Isles shall be recognised unless it first be sanctioned and recommended by the Association.

69. Contracting Out

No club or club management committee or any individual shall have the right or power to contract out of any of the Laws of the Game.

REGULATING SINGLE-HANDED PAIRS AND TRIPLES GAMES

70. The foregoing Laws, where applicable, shall also apply to single-handed, pairs and triples games.

SPECTATORS

71. Persons not engaged in the game shall be situate clear of and beyond the limits of the rink of play, and clear of banks. They shall neither by word nor act disturb or advise the players.

This second sentence does not apply as regards advice GIVEN FROM THE BANK from a non-playing Captain or a Manager of the team or side.

The setting up of Betting Stands on the premises of Affiliated Clubs in connection with any game or games shall not be permitted.

DUTIES OF MARKER

72.(a) The Marker shall control the game in accordance with these Laws. He shall, before play commences, examine all bowls for the imprint of the Official Stamp, such imprint to be clearly visible, and shall ascertain by measurement the width of the rink of play.

(b) He shall centre the jack, and shall place a full length jack two yards (1.8 metres) from the ditch.

(c) He shall ensure that the jack is not less than 25 yards (22.86 metres) from the front edge of the mat, after it has been centred.

(d) He shall stand at one side of the rink, and to the rear of the jack.

(e) He shall answer affirmatively or negatively a player's inquiry as to whether a bowl is jack high. If requested, he shall indicate the distance of any bowl from the jack, or from any other bowl, and also, if requested, indicate which bowl he thinks is shot and/or the relative position of any other bowl.

(f) Subject to contrary directions from either opponent under Law 34, he shall mark all 'touchers' immediately they come to rest, and remove chalk marks from non-touchers. With the agreement of both opponents he shall remove all dead bowls from the green and the ditch. He shall mark the positions of the jack and 'touchers' which are in the ditch. (See Laws 33 and 40).

(g) He shall not move, or cause to be moved, either jack or bowls until each player has agreed to the number of shots.

(h) He shall measure carefully all doubtful shots when requested by either player. If unable to come to a decision satisfactory to the players, he shall call in an Umpire. If an official Umpire has not been appointed, the marker shall select one. The decision of the Umpire shall be final.

(i) He shall enter the score at each end, and shall intimate to the players the state of the game. When the game is finished, he shall see that the score card, containing the names of the players, is signed by the players, and disposed of in accordance with the rules of the competition.

DUTIES OF UMPIRE

73. An Umpire shall be appointed by the English Bowls Umpires Association, or the Controlling Body, whether it be Council, Association, Club or Tournament Committee. His duties shall be as follows:

(a) He shall examine all bowls for the imprint of the IBB Stamp, or that of its National Association, and ascertain by measurement the width of the rinks of play.

(b) He shall measure any shot or shots in dispute, and for this purpose shall use a suitable measure. His decision shall be final.

(c) He shall decide all questions as to the distance of the mat from the ditch, and the jack from the mat.

(d) He shall decide as to whether or not jack and/or bowls are in play.

(e) He shall enforce the Laws of the Game.

(f) In Championships and International Matches the Umpire's decision shall be final in respect of any breach of a Law, except that, upon questions relating to the meaning or interpretation of any Law there shall be a right of appeal to the Controlling Body.

PLAYERS' STATUS AND INVOLVEMENT

Any player may participate in any event for reward in cash or kind.

An amateur player is one who plays the game wholly as a non-remunerative or non-profit making sport or pastime.

To maintain his amateur status the recipient of such rewards may deduct his expenses as defined below but must remit the balance to the Governing Body concerned.

(a) Assistance administered through his National Association for:
The cost of food and lodging;
The cost of transport;
Pocket money to cover incidental expenses;
The expenses for insurance cover in respect of accidents, illness, personal property and disability;
The purchase of personal clothing and sports equipment;
The cost of medical treatment, physiotherapy and authorised coaches.

(b) Compensation authorised by the National Authority concerned in case of necessity to cover financial loss from his absence from work or basic occupation. In no circumstances shall payment made under this provision exceed the sum the player would have earned in his work in the same periods. The compensation may be paid with the approval of the National Authority concerned.

STAMPING OF BOWLS

Each bowl complying with the requirements of Law 9 of these Laws shall be stamped with the official stamp of the IBB, BIBC or that of its National Association. The currency of the stamp shall be for a period of 15 (fifteen) years expiring on 31 December and the imprint on the bowl shall record the latest year in which such bowl may be validly used.

The EIBA reserves the right to make its own arrangements for testing and stamping of bowls where this is considered necessary. Provided that bowls comply with Law 9 of these Laws and bear a current official stamp, such bowls may also be validly used in Championship and International Matches.

The EIBA have decided that bowls bearing a legible stamp of 1971 or later can continue to be used without restamping until the stamp becomes illegible. (This decision applies to composition bowls only for indoor play, and bowls will have to be stamped as heretofore for outdoor play).

Stamping of Bowls

Manufacturers will be entitled to use an oval IBB stamp, to facilitate the imprint between the inner and outer rings of bowls. Imprints on running surfaces should be avoided wherever possible.

Metric Equivalents

In connection with the manufacture of bowls there is no objection to manufacturers using metric equivalents in lieu of the present figures, always provided that Law 9 of the Board's Laws is complied with. Furthermore, there is no objection to manufacturers indicating various sizes of Bowls by numerals, and the manufactuers will be entitled to use the following table if they so desire.

Size in inches	Size Number	Actual Metric (mm)	May be rounded off Metric (mm)
$4^5/_8$	0	117.4	117
$4^3/_4$	1	120.7	121
$4^{13}/_{16}$	2	122.2	122
$4^7/_8$	3	123.8	124
$4^{15}/_{16}$	4	125.4	125
5	5	127.0	127
$5^1/_{16}$	6	128.6	129
$5^1/_8$	7	130.2	130

If size numbers are utilised and size measurements omitted, then no bowl in diameter shall be less than $4^5/_8$ inches (117.4 mm) nor more than $5^1/_8$ inches (130.2 mm) and no bowl shall weigh more than 3 lbs 8 oz (1.6 kg).

It is the responsibility of all players, Umpires and markers to refrain at all times from committing any act which is liable in any way to cause damage to the indoor green or carpet.

Reproduced by kind permission of the English Bowling Association. 1985 edition.

THE SHORT MAT GAME

MAT MEASUREMENTS

RINK MAT
Max. Length	45'
Min. Length	40'
Width	6'
Width Tolerance	2"

FENDER
Back
6' (Inside) × 3" × 3"
Sides
12" (Inside) × 3" × 3"

BLOCK
Length	15"
Height	3"
Max. Width	3"

DELIVERY MAT
Length	24"
Width	14"

DELIVERY LINES
From centre line	13"
From ditch line	4'6"

DELIVERY MAT LINES
From centre line	7"
Length	12"

DITCH LINE
From fender	12"

DEAD LINE
From ditch line	9'

JACK LINE
From dead line	3'
From ditch line	3'

BLOCK LINE
Length	15"

MARKINGS
White
  adhesive tape   ½"

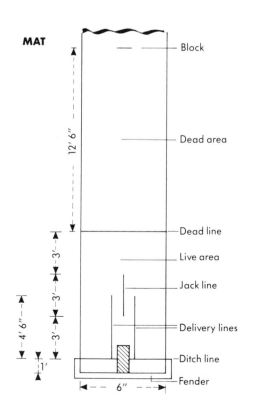

DEFINITIONS AND GLOSSARY

Backhand to the right-handed player is the delivery to the left hand side of the block.

To the left-handed player it is the delivery to the right hand side of the block.

Bias is the peculiar property of one side of the bowl, caused by shaping which enables it to follow a curved course.

Block means the obstacle which is placed midway between each end of the rink mat on the block line.

Blocking means covering the lying shot or jack with a guarding bowl in order to hinder an opponent.

Bowl in course means a bowl from the time of delivery until it comes to rest.

Controlling body means the body having immediate control of the conditions under which the match is played.

Dead Area means that section of the rink mat between the dead lines.

Delivery Lines means the markings within which the players' feet are restricted to deliver the bowl.

Delivery Mat means the foot-mat upon which the stance is taken to deliver the bowl.

Displaced or Disturbed means accidentally moving a bowl or jack otherwise than by a bowl in play.

Draw means delivering the bowl with sufficient impetus to reach its objective with the necessary green to allow the bias to take effect.

End means the placing and playing to the jack and the playing of all the players' bowls in the same direction on the rink mat.

Fender means the surround that encloses the ditch.

Forehand to the right-handed player is the delivery to the right hand side of the block.

To the left-handed player it is the delivery to the left hand side of the block.

Four means four players on one side whose position of playing are called Lead, Second, Third and Skip.

Head means the jack and such bowls as have come to rest within the boundary of the rink mat and are not dead.

Jack high means that the nearest portion of the bowl referred to is the same distance from the dead line as the nearest portion of the jack.

Lead means the player on each side who plays first.

Live Area means that section of the rink mat between the dead line and the ditch line, delineated by the edge of the half-inch marking.

Pair means two players on one side whose position in order of playing are Lead and Skip.

Rink Mat means the whole rectangular playing surface.

Running Wood means a bowl delivered with sufficient impetus to prevent its bias from taking full effect . . . (used for removing a bowl or breaking the head).

Skip means the player who controls the play on behalf of his side on any rink mat.

Singles means one player competing against another.

Team means any agreed number of players on one side.

Touchers is the term applied to a bowl which touches the live jack while the bowl is in motion on the rink mat and before it comes to rest.

It shall also be a toucher if the said bowl deflects off a bowl at rest or the jack is sprung to touch the bowl whilst it is still in motion or if it falls and touches the jack before the next bowl has been delivered.

The toucher will remain in play until the end is completed even when in the ditch . . . it shall be indicated by a chalk mark which should be placed on it before the next bowl comes to rest . . . if this is impractical because there is danger of the bowl falling over or moving, it shall be nominated and chalked when the danger has passed.

Trailing means contacting the jack with sufficient momentum so to move it and follow it to the new position.

Triple means any three players on one side whose position of playing are called Lead, Second and Skip.

Wick is the term applied to a bowl which glances off another bowl or bowls so as to change its natural line of travel.

EQUIPMENT

1. The Rink Mat:
(a) **Description.** The rink mat shall be of a suitable material conducive to the true running of the bowls as approved by the ESMBA.

It shall be coloured green and shall have a suitable underlay or an approved bonded backing.

The maximum length shall be 45 feet and the minimum length 40 feet including ditches. The width shall be 6 feet with a tolerance of 2 inches.

The floor surface should be level.
(b) **Markings.** The rink mat shall be marked with half inch lines which must be white in colour.

The lines may be affixed by adhesive, painted on or woven into the material.
(c) **Ditch and deadlines.** Lines representing the ditch shall be marked across each end of the rink mat one foot from the fender and similar transverse lines shall be marked nine feet from each line to represent the dead lines.
(d) **Jack Line.** The jack line shall be three feet long and in the middle of the rink mat with one end three feet from the ditch line and the other end three feet from the dead line.
(e) **Delivery Lines.** Delivery lines shall be marked four feet six inches long starting at right-angles from the ditch line and the distance on each side from the centre line of the rink mat shall be thirteen inches.
(f) **Delivery Mat Lines.** Delivery mat lines shall be marked twelve inches long starting at right-angles from the ditch line towards the fender and the distance on each side from the centre line of the rink mat shall be seven inches.
(g) **Block Line.** The block line shall be fifteen inches long and centred across the centre of the rink mat.

2. Delivery Mat: The delivery mat shall be twenty-four inches long and fourteen inches wide.

3. Ditch and Fender: The width of the ditch shall be twelve inches. It shall be enclosed at the back and both sides with a fender three inches high and not more than three inches wide. It shall be coloured white and must not be covered with any material.

4. The Block: The block shall be fifteen inches long, three inches high and not more than three inches wide. It shall be coloured white and must not be covered by material.

5. The Bowls:
(a) Bowls shall not exceed 5¼ inches or be less than 4½ inches diameter and shall not exceed 3½ lb in weight.
(b) Loading of bowls is strictly prohibited.
(c) Coloured discs or stickers may be used to identify team or club bowls and for this purpose they shall be classed as part of that bowl. The placing of a number of stickers on top of each other could render that bowl invalid if objected to.
(d) Bias 3 bowls are recommended.

6. The Jack: The jack shall be round and white and be made of a material approved by the ESMBA. Its diameter shall not be less than 2½ inches or more than 2¾ inches. It shall weigh not less than eight ounces or more than fifteen ounces.

Heavyweight jacks are preferred.

7. Footwear: Bowling shoes or any smooth heelless footwear must be worn while playing on the rink mat.

8. Dress Regulations: Where dress regulations are stipulated for any match, championship or event . . . NO PERSON SHALL PARTICIPATE IF IMPROPERLY DRESSED.

CONDITIONS OF THE GAME

9. Form and Duration: A game of bowls shall be played on one rink mat or on several rink mats. It shall consist of a specified number of shots or ends or shall be played for any period of time as previously arranged.

10. Play Arrangements:
(a) A game shall be played on one rink mat as:
  (i) A singles game by two players, each player playing two, three or four bowls singly and alternately.
  (ii) A pairs game by two players on either side, each playing two, three or four bowls.

  The two leads shall play all their bowls singly alternately and in turn before changing ends with the skips who will then bowl their bowls alternately and in turn.

  (iii) A triples game by two teams of three players on each side, each player playing two or three bowls singly, alternately and in turn with the leads playing all their bowls before the seconds be allowed to bowl their bowls.

  The leads will remain at the mat end until after both seconds have bowled all their bowls, then these four players will change ends with the skips who will now bowl their bowls singly, alternately and in turn.

  (iv) A fours game by four players on either side who shall be called lead, second, third and skip according to the position and order in which they play.

  Each player will play two bowls only, each singly, alternately and in turn, the leads will play both their bowls before the seconds be allowed to bowl theirs and all players shall remain behind the mat until both thirds have bowled all their bowls then all players will change ends with the skips who will now bowl their bowls, singly, alternately and in turn.

(b) A team game shall be played by two sides on a given number of rink mats, each side composed of an equal number of players.

GENERAL CONDITIONS OF PLAY

11. Trial Ends: Trial ends shall be at the discretion of the controlling body.

12. Tossing for start:
(a) The captains in a team game shall toss; the winner has the option to play first or second on all rink mats.
(b) In games played on one rink mat, the leads shall toss and the winner shall have the option of playing first or second.

13. Playing first:
(a) In all subsequent ends to the first, the winner of the preceding end shall play first.
(b) In the event of a tied end (no score) or a dead end, the player who played first in that end shall again play first.

14. Placing the Delivery Mat:
(a) At the beginning of an end the player who is to play first shall place the delivery mat within the delivery mat lines, with the shorter side in contact with the fender.
(b) The delivery mat must not be moved until the end is complete. If accidentally moved it must be returned to its proper position by the following player.
(c) The last player to bowl in that end shall remove the delivery mat clear of the rink mat.

15. Placing the Jack:
(a) The marker in a singles game shall place the jack on the jack line where the player who is to play first requires it.
(b) The skip whose side it is to play first shall place the jack on the jack line at any length he chooses.

16. Stance on the Delivery Mat: A player at the moment of delivering his bowl shall have one foot entirely within the confines of the delivery mat. The foot must be either in contact with or directly above the delivery mat and the other foot must be inside the delivery lines. Failure to observe this Law constitutes foot faulting.

17. Foot Faulting:

(a) Should a player in a singles game foot-fault the marker shall stop the bowl and remove it clear of the rink mat.

(b) The opposing skip shall stop and remove the offending bowl.

18. Fender Displacement:

(a) Should the fender become displaced in a singles game, the marker will replace it and restore the jack or any bowls which may have moved to their original position.

(b) The opposing skip shall be responsible for restoring the jack and any bowls to their original position if he is at the head end, if not this duty will be carried out by the player who is controlling the play on his behalf.

THE BOWLS

19. A Live Bowl is:

(a) A bowl which in its original course comes to rest within the live area.

(b) A bowl which in its original course breaks the ditch line but does not interfere with any toucher or the jack in the ditch, or touch the fender or makes contact with the floor or the block and comes to rest in the live area.

(c) A bowl which in its original course on the rink mat touches the jack, either directly or by deflection off another bowl or bowls, even though it settles in the ditch or makes contact with the fender after it has touched the jack, such a bowl shall be live and be called a toucher.

20. Marking a Toucher:

(a) A toucher shall be clearly marked with chalk by a member of the players side before the next bowl delivered comes to rest. If a bowl is not so marked before the succeeding bowl comes to rest it will cease to be a toucher.

If in the opinion of either skip or the player in charge of the head that to attempt to chalk such a bowl could cause it to fall or move, it shall not be chalked but it must be nominated as a toucher and it should then be chalked

if the danger ceases during the course of play.

(b) The marker in a singles game should chalk all touchers and should indicate to the players any bowl which is a toucher that he is unable to mark.

(c) Should a bowl be played which has not had the chalk mark removed, the skip, the player in charge of the head or the marker shall remove the mark as soon as the bowl comes to rest, or if there is a danger that such a bowl should fall and alter the head or its position, it should be indicated and the mark removed if the position is changed.

(d) All toucher marks should be removed before any bowl is played.

21. Action of Touchers:

(a) Touchers may 'act upon the jack or other touchers in the ditch. The jack and any such touchers moved shall remain in their new position.

(b) Touchers rebounding from the jack or the fender or from other touchers in the ditch onto the live area, shall remain in play where they have come to rest.

22. Dead Bowls: A bowl is dead and must be removed from the rink mat if:

(a) It is delivered from a foot-fault position.

(b) It strikes the block or passes over it.

(c) It does not travel beyond the dead area.

(d) It finishes in the ditch without touching the jack.

(e) It touches or rebounds from the fender or contacts a toucher or the jack which is in the ditch.

(f) If any portion of the bowl intersects any part of the dead line.

(g) When it comes to rest and any portion of it intersects any part of the ditch line, unless it is a toucher.

(h) It makes contact with the floor or leaves the rink mat.

23. Underlay: The underlay is part of the playing surface.

24. Line Decisions: All line decisions must be dealt with before the next bowl is played . . . failure to comply with this rule will render such bowl live.

25. Bowl Displacement:

(a) Displacement by a non-toucher.
A head is disturbed by:
  (i) A bowl delivered from a foot-fault position.
  (ii) A bowl which strikes or contacts the block.
  (iii) A bowl which rebounds from a toucher which is in the ditch.
  (iv) A bowl deflected by the fender.
  (v) A bowl or jack in the ditch which is moved by a non-toucher.

It shall be restored as near as possible to its original position by the opposing skip or by the player who is in charge of play at the head, and the end completed.

(b) Displacement by a participating player.
  If a bowl while in motion or at rest on the rink mat, or if a toucher in the ditch, be interfered with or displaced by one of the players, the opposing skip shall have the option of:
  (i) Restoring the bowl as near as possible to its original position.
  (ii) Letting it remain in its new position.
  (iii) Declaring the bowl dead and remove it from the rink mat.
  (iv) Playing the end again, and it must be from the same direction.

(c) Displacement by a non-player.
  If a bowl while in motion or at rest on the rink mat, or if a toucher in the ditch, be interfered with or be displaced by any person not playing, or by a jack or bowl from another rink mat or by any other object; the two skips will come to an agreement regarding its original position.
  Should the skips fail to agree, the end shall be played again in the same direction.

(d) Displacement by the marker.
  If a bowl is moved as it is being marked or measured by the marker, it shall be restored as near as possible to its original position by the marker, subject to the agreement by both players.
  If the players cannot agree, the end shall be played again from the same direction.
  If shot or shots have already been awarded, the player holding the shots will have the option of accepting this as the score for that end or playing the end again.

(e) Displacement by the umpire.
  If the umpire accidentally moves the jack or bowl while measuring, he will replace it as near as possible to its original position before completing his decision.
  He will be sole arbiter in the matter.

THE JACK

26. A jack is live and may be played by a live bowl if the jack is within the live area, or if any portion of it is within the live area when it is intersecting the ditch line.

27. A jack driven into the ditch shall be live and shall not be moved except by a toucher.

28. Dead Jack: The jack is dead if:
  (a) Any portion of it comes in direct contact with the floor or any other non-playing surface other than the fender.
  NOTE: The underlay is part of the playing surface.
  (b) It is driven by a bowl in play beyond the boundary of the rink mat i.e.: over the fender, off the side, or over the dead line.
  (c) After rebounding it comes to rest either in the dead area or with any portion of it intersecting the dead line.

29. Dead End: When the jack is dead it will not be counted as an end, even if all the bowls in that end have been played.
  The end will be played again and must be played from the same direction.

30. Rebounding Jack: Should the jack be driven against the fender and rebound on to the live area, or should it rebound from a toucher in the ditch on to the live area, or after being played into the ditch it be moved by a toucher so as to find its way on to the live area, it shall be played to in the same manner as if it never left the live area.

31. Jack Displacement:
  (a) Displacement by a non-toucher.

A jack disturbed by a bowl which:
  (i) has been delivered from a foot-fault position.
  (ii) strikes or touches the block.
  (iii) being a non-toucher rebounds from the fender.
  (iv) being a non-toucher contacts it in the ditch.
It shall be restored as near as possible to its original position by the opposing skip or by the player in charge of the head for him.

(b) Displacement by a participating player:
If the jack which is in motion or at rest on the rink mat be interfered with by a player, the opponent skip shall have the option of:
  (i) Restoring the jack as near as possible to its original position.
  (ii) Letting it remain where it now rests.
  (iii) Playing the end again from the same direction.

(c) Displacement by a non-player.
If the jack while in motion or at rest on the rink mat, be interfered with, displaced or moved by a non-player, or by a jack or bowl from another rink mat or by any other object, the skips shall come to an agreement regarding its original position and the jack will be restored.

Should they fail to agree, that end will be played again and it must be from the same direction.

(d) Displacement by the marker.
If the jack is moved by the marker whilst measuring it will be replaced as near as possible to its original position and both players will agree its position, if they do not agree then the end will be replayed from the same direction.

If a shot or shots have already been agreed that player shall have the right to accept that score.

(e) Displacement by a player measuring.
Should a player in the act of measuring accidentally move the jack, the opposing player who agrees the shots shall:
  (i) Replace the jack as near as possible to its original position.
  (ii) Agree the shot or shots already claimed.
  (iii) Agree or accept the shot or shots already taken out.
  (iv) Play the end again from the same direction.

(f) Displacement by the umpire.
Should the umpire accidentally move the jack whilst in the act of measuring, he will replace it in its original position before completing his decision . . . He will be the sole arbiter of the position and his decision shall be binding.

32. Possession of the Rink Mat:

(a) Possession of the rink mat shall belong to the side whose bowl is being played.
(b) The players in possession of the rink mat shall not be interfered with, annoyed, barracked, or have their attention distracted by their opponents.
(c) As soon as each bowl has come to rest, possession of the rink mat shall be transferred to the other side, time being allowed for marking a toucher, removing dead bowls or making line decisions.

33. Position of Players:
Players not in the act of playing or controlling play must stand clear of the rink mat and be behind the fender.

34. Players and their Duties:
Skip
(a) The skip shall have sole charge of his side, he will control the play and his instructions must be obeyed by all his players.
(b) With the opposing skip he will decide all disputed points or shots, when both skips agree their decision shall be final.

If they cannot agree either one will call the umpire who will then arbitrate and his decision shall be final and binding.

In the absence of an official umpire, any person mutually agreed by both players will arbitrate and his decision will be final and binding.
(c) He will be responsible for marking all touchers or removing the chalk mark from any non-touchers. He will be responsible for removing any dead bowls from the ditch, off the rink mat or dead area.

(d) He will decide on any line bowls with the other skip and any other matters or will call the umpire to adjudicate.

(c) While at the playing end he may visit the head only when in possession of the rink mat. He will not carry his bowl beyond the nearest dead line . . . any bowl so carried beyond the dead line will be declared dead and must be removed from the rink mat.

Third in a Fours Game

(a) The third will do all measuring and agreeing the shots or shot, allowing the opposite number also to measure and will inform the skip of the result.

If either third cannot agree they will call the skips who will then arbitrate.

(b) The third will mark all touchers or remove the marks from any non-toucher and will remove any dead bowls from the rink mat or the ditch, and will see that the jack or any toucher in the ditch is not disturbed except by another toucher.

(c) The third will take charge of the head only when the side is in possession of the rink mat . . . If the head is changed he will inform the skip and direct the play accordingly.

(d) The third may remain up at the head end while the leads and seconds are bowling their bowls at the discretion of the controlling body.

Second in a Fours Game

(a) The second will keep the scorecard and will see the names of all players on each side are entered.

(b) The second will record the score both for and against as agreed by the thirds and will compare the card with the opposing second after each end.

(c) The second will be responsible for the scorecard and will retain it in his/her possession at all times and hand it to the skip on completion.

Second in a Triples Game

(a) The second will keep the scorecard as in a fours game but will also agree the shot or shots with the opposing second, and having recorded them will inform the skip.

(b) The second will prove the claim for

shot or shots by measuring but will not cause any bowl to be moved until the shot or shots are agreed, allowing the opposing second also to measure, and if they cannot agree will call the skip to arbitrate.

(c) The second will take charge of the head only when their side is in possession of the rink mat and will inform the skip if the head has been altered and guide the play accordingly.

(d) the second will chalk all touchers and remove the marks from any non-touchers.

(e) The second will remove any dead bowls from the ditch.

(f) The second will see that the jack or any toucher in the ditch is not disturbed except by the action of another toucher.

(g) The second will not visit the head whilst at the delivery mat end and will remain behind the mat until the opposing second has bowled all their bowls in that end.

Leads

(a) The lead shall place the delivery mat correctly and see that the jack is correctly centred on the jack line before playing the first bowl.

(b) The leads shall bowl singly and alternately until all their bowls have been played.

(c) The leads will not visit the head or go to the head end until all the other players at that end have bowled all their bowls and will remain behind the delivery mat or the fender.

35. Play Infringements: Following the bowl up the Rink Mat

No player shall follow their bowl up to the head on the rink mat or leave the rink mat and follow it up the side.

Any player who infringes this law must be warned as soon as they cross the nearest dead line and on the second offence the opposing skip can have the bowl stopped and removed from the rink mat or have the end played again but it must be from the same direction.

NOTE. This does not apply to the skips who may visit the head.

Playing before the last Bowl has come to rest

(a) A bowl played before the last bowl has come to rest must be stopped and removed from the rink mat.

(b) Any such bowl played that disturbs the head or makes contact with any bowl or the jack; the opponent may leave the head as altered or declare it void.

It will be replayed from the same direction.

Changing the order of Play

Players may change their order of play at the completion of any end.

Playing out of turn

(a) If a player plays before their turn the opposing skip shall have the right to stop the bowl and cause it to be played again in its proper order.

(b) If a bowl so played has moved the jack or altered the head; the opposing skip shall have the option of allowing the head to remain as it is or to declare it void.

(c) If the head is declared void, it will be replayed from the same direction.

(d) If the head is allowed to remain in its new position, the other players will follow in the new order of play.

Playing the wrong Bowl

A bowl played by mistake shall be replaced by the players own bowl.

Changing Bowls

No player shall change their bowls during a game unless they become damaged or objected to as not complying with the Laws.

Leaving the Rink Mat

(a) No player will leave the rink mat while a game is in progress without first consulting their opposite number, and then for a period not exceeding 10 minutes.

(b) If during a team game a player is forced to leave a game through illness or other just cause, their place may be taken by a substitute if both team captains agree.

(c) Should the sick or indisposed player return after substitute has joined the players at the rink mat, even though the substitute had not bowled, the player will not be allowed to rejoin the game, nor can he/she act as substitute in any other set.

(d) Should the opposing team captain not agree to playing a substitute or should there not be a substitute available, the game will continue with the missing player being classed as the second.

Absentee Players

(a) If a player is absent from a side at the time laid down for the commencement of the game, a wait of 10 minutes may be allowed.

(b) If trial ends are to be played, they will take place, the missing player will forfeit his or her rights to trial ends.

(c) If the missing player arrives before the trial ends are completed they will be allowed to play. Only the trial ends will be forfeited.

(d) If the missing player has not arrived by the expiry of the time allowed, a singles or a pairs game will be awarded to the opponents.

(e) A triples or fours game will commence with the missing player being considered as the second and a definite order of play will be maintained, it shall be Lead, Lead, Second, Lead, Lead, Second.

(f) If the missing player arrives after the delivery mat has been placed for the first end, they will not be allowed to play.

Playing with a Player missing

There will be no penalty or extra bowls played by the side with a player missing, but in a triples or fours game the missing player will be considered as the second and a definite order of play will be maintained, it shall be: Lead, Lead, Second, Lead, Lead, Second.

Objects on the Rink Mat

Under no circumstances shall any object to assist any player or to influence the play, be placed on the rink mat or on the fender, or on the jack, or on a bowl or elsewhere.

36. Results of an End: The Shot or Shots

(a) A shot or shots shall be adjudged by

the bowl or bowls nearer the jack than the nearest bowl played by the opposite side.

(b) When the last bowl of the end comes to rest, 30 seconds shall elapse if either side requests it, during that time no bowls shall be touched, chalked up, measured or interfered with. The request must be made as soon as the last bowl has come to rest.

(c) Neither the jack or bowls must be moved until both sides agree the result, except where a bowl or bowls have to be removed to allow another to be measured.

(d) No measuring shall be allowed until after the last bowl has come to rest.

Measuring

(a) All measuring must be done with calipers, flexible measure or other equipment approved by the ESMBA.

(b) All measuring shall be to the nearest point of both objects.

(c) If a bowl requiring to be measured is resting on another bowl which prevents it being measured, the best means available shall be taken to secure it in position, whereupon the other bowl shall be removed . . . the same applies if more than one bowl is involved.

The use of the hand or the finger for this purpose is prohibited.

(d) The same applies if a bowl not so resting is in danger of falling before measuring is complete.

(e) The placing of the hand or finger on the jack or on any bowl to be measured constitutes disturbance and the opposing side shall claim the shot or shots or refuse to acknowledge the shot or shots in dispute.

(f) Measuring with hand, foot, mat or any other object other than the recognised measure is prohibited.

Live End No Score

When at the conclusion of an end the nearest bowl of each side are touching the jack or the two nearest bowls are of an equal distance from the jack, or there are no bowls in the live area or touchers in the ditch; it shall be deemed to be a live end and no score, the end shall be recorded as a

played end.

The player who played first in that tied end shall again play first and it shall be played from where the last end finished.

37. **Extra End**

(a) In the event of a draw at the conclusion of the game where a winner must be determined, an extra end must be played.

(b) The team captains in a team game or the leads in other games shall toss for start, the winner shall have the right to play first or second.

(c) The extra end shall be played from where the last end finished.

(d) If at the conclusion of the extra end it is still a draw a further extra end will be played, the toss will again be made and the end played from where the last end finished.

38. **Game Decisions:** The winner is the player or team with the highest number of shots or points at the end of the game.

39. **Spectators:** Persons not engaged in the game shall be situated clear of and beyond the limits of the rink mat.

They shall neither by word or act disturb or advise the players.

The officials shall have the power to take what action is necessary to control any spectators.

DUTIES OF THE MARKER

40. **The marker shall:**

(a) be familiar with the ESMBA Laws of the Game and see such Laws are complied with.

(b) be in possession of a reliable measure, calipers and chalk.

(c) be in possession of the scorecard and pen or pencil, and will see the names of both contestants are entered.

(d) make themselves familiar with the identifying marks on the bowls of each player.

(e) witness the toss for the start.

(f) see the mat is correctly aligned and will place the jack on the jack line at the position required by the player to bowl first.

(g) observe a strict neutrality.

(h) answer any questions put to them by the players but will not give any information unless requested.

(i) not pass any comment.

(j) address only the person who has possession of the rink mat.

(k) record only the score as agreed by the players.

(l) measure only when requested but will not cause any bowl to be moved until both players agree the shot or shots.

(m) in any difficult measure not to attempt to make a decision but will call the umpire to adjudicate.

(n) keep the players informed as to the state of the game.

(o) mark all touchers and remove the marks from any non-touchers.

(p) remove all dead bowls from the ditch and the dead area.

(q) adjudicate on all line bowls.

(r) on completion of the game see that the scorecard is signed by the losing player and handed in to the game controller or official.

41. Duties of the Umpire

(a) enforce the ESMBA Laws of the Game.

(b) see that the game is continuous and played in a competitive and sporting manner.

(c) be available for consultation on any matter or point of Law concerning the game.

(d) measure all difficult shots when requested, he/she will tolerate no interference and his decision is final and binding.

(e) arbitrate in any dispute and his/her decision is final.

(f) pass no comment, advice or praise.

(g) remain strictly neutral and unbiased at all time.

Note: There shall be nothing in these Laws which prevents any player from playing for cash or kind or any other reward. Nor shall they prohibit cash or kind being offered.

Appendix II
Glossary of Terms

In this Appendix I explain the main terms used by bowlers. Various cross-references are included, but this section should not be confused with the separate Index.

Where reference is made in this section to the Laws of the game, these Laws are those relating to the outdoor Lawn Bowls game.

Arc The curved path taken by the bowl owing to its bias. This path becomes more curved (inwards towards the bias) as the momentum of the bowl decreases.

Athletic stance An upright stance on the mat prior to and during the initial stage of delivery. As opposed to the crouch stance or the fixed stance.

Backhand (delivery) A delivery to the left of the central line in the case of a right-handed player or to the right in the case of the left-handed bowler.

Back wood(s) A bowl or bowls lying to the rear of the jack and usually well behind the main part of the head. It is often good policy to have some back woods so that, if the jack is moved back, a rear bowl can become shot.

Bank The raised area around the green behind the ditch.

Be up An appeal (or order!) to deliver your bowls up to or beyond the jack and *not* short of the target where they will hinder following players. In general 'Be up' is very good advice – a player failing to comply will not be popular.

Bias The action of the specially constructed bowl which causes it to turn in a slight arc and not run in a straight line. There are degrees of bias and several changing factors affect the degree of bias.

Bias markings The smaller rings (or discs or emblems) on the side of a bowl signifying the bias side to which it will turn as speed is lost. The bias markings must always be on the inside, nearer the jack, as you take your angled stance on the mat.

Block A bowl deliberately (or accidentally!) delivered well short of the jack with the object of blocking the line of approach of an opponent's bowl or causing him to change from his favoured line of delivery.

In the Short-Mat game, the wooden bar placed centrally across the mat to stop drives.

Boundary The playing area of a rink as defined by the string or imaginary lines running from the boundary pegs and up to the rear of the end ditches.

Bowl(s) The nearly circular ball-like object which is delivered onto the rink in such a manner as to make it roll to the jack. The modern bowl is made of composition and is produced in matching sets of four in various sizes, weights and styles.

Bumper A bad delivery in which the bowl is released from the hand well above the grass or carpet level, resulting in a distinct bump.

Cannon As in billiards or snooker, the action of one bowl hitting and bouncing off another so as to alter its running line.

Cant The action of tilting the bowl slightly in the hand on delivery. This can alter the degree of bias to some degree according to the direction of tilt. This is not recommended practice for the new player.

Cast The act of delivering the jack from the mat.

Centre-line The imaginary line running down the middle of each rink from one rink number marker to the other. The jack should be centred to this line which can now be marked at each end.

Chalked A bowl which has hit the jack during its delivery, and is therefore a 'toucher', is so designated by being chalked.

Claw grip One of the three basic methods of holding the bowl before and during delivery.

Cot Name for the jack, as sometimes used in East Anglia.

Count The total of scoring bowls at the completion of an end. This has to be agreed by both sides.

Cradle grip One of the three basic methods of holding the Bowl before and during delivery.

Crouch stance The body during and before the delivery action is slightly doubled up or crouched. The arm and the bowl are therefore nearer the grass than they would be with the athletic stance.

Dead The expression used for a bowl or jack which has been delivered or later moved out of the field of play as defined in the Laws. An end can also be declared dead.

Dead bowl A bowl becomes 'dead' if it travels less than 15 yards from the front of the mat, if it comes to rest (initially or later) totally over the side-string or boundary of the rink, if it over-runs the end into (or beyond) the ditch without first touching the jack, or if it rebounds from the bank not being a toucher.

A dead bowl cannot be counted in the score and must be removed from the rink to the top of the bank.

Dead draw An extremely accurate draw with the bowl resting against the jack. Dead lucky in some cases!

Dead end An end which has become void, perhaps because the jack has been knocked out of the side confines of the rink. This end is not counted and is played again.

Dead green An extremely slow green perhaps the result of over-long or wet grass.

Dead jack A jack no longer in play, probably because it has been driven completely over the boundary lines of the rink. Other reasons include the jack being driven over the bank or rebounding back down the rink to rest less than 22 yards from the front of the mat. The jack is also dead if on delivery it fails to travel 25 yards (after centring) from the mat, or ends up in the ditch on its initial delivery.

Delivery The act of delivering the bowl from a static position to its forward propulsion down the rink in a smooth continuous movement.

Disc A small round addition on the bias side of the bowl. Its purpose is to mark this side and to identify in an unique manner a player's bowl.

Displaced bowl A bowl impeded in its run or subsequently moved or interfered with by any person.

Displaced jack A jack which is moved by a bowl and which remains in play within the confines of the rink or end ditch is not, of course, re-centred but is played to in its new position.

Ditch The recessed gutter surrounding the green or more importantly situated at the end of each rink.

Ditch rink The rink nearest to the side ditches. There will be two such rinks on each green. These can play unevenly or even have a slight tilt due to extra wear when the line of play is across the green. Also called an **End rink.**

Draw (a) The basic shot, directed at the jack, to rest your bowl nearer to this target than that of your opponents; or (b) the line needed to be taken by a bowl to end dead centre on the rink.

Draw shot The basic bowling shot where the bowl comes to rest against the jack.

Drawn end If it is impossible to determine which side's bowl is closer to the jack, the end may be declared drawn. No score is entered but the end shall be counted as having been played.

Drive An aggressive shot, a very fast delivery made to destroy a head, to move an opposing bowl or jack. Not recommended for the novice player. Sometimes called a **Firing shot.**

Duggler Apparently a term used when a bowl rests against the jack.

Duster A necessary accessory for wiping the bowls before delivery. Also much used by skips (or number threes) for indicating to the bowler the line of approach to be taken.

End Each complete game starting from the casting of the jack to the time when each player has delivered all his bowls and the score has been decided.

End rink See **Ditch rink**

Extra end The additional end which may need to be played in an eliminating competition when the score is tied at the completion of the agreed or regulation number of ends. In this case the captains or skips have to toss to determine which side leads and the mat is placed as for the first end.

Fast green A surface on which the bowl will run for a longer period and distance than normal, usually because it is dry and closely cropped. The bowl will take a wide curve and require more land or green than on a **Slow green.** Speeds of 14 seconds or more would be termed fast in the British Isles.

Federation This version of the game played in some 12 counties in the Eastern part of the country under English Bowling Federation Laws differs in some respects from the standard version. For example, there are no ditches and the players in a team can change their playing position in the team, but the basic art of bowls remains the same.

Finger-grip One of three basic methods of holding the bowl before and during delivery.

Firing shot See **Drive**

Firm shot A delivery with rather more weight than would be required to draw level with the jack. This is normally employed like a 'yard-on' shot when one is seeking to displace an opposing bowl.

Fixed stance A stance where one foot is placed down the delivery line before the swing and delivery is commenced.

Fluke A lucky shot which has an unexpected result, usually on account of a chance wick, deflection or cannon.

Follow-on A bowl delivered with enough momentum or top-spin to enable it to displace other bowls and then continue its course to rest near the jack.

Follow-through The continuing forward swing of the arm and body after the point when the bowl has left the hand and is grassed.

Foot fault At the point of delivery of the bowl from your hand, at least one of your feet must be entirely on, or over, the mat. If this is not so, it is a foot fault.

Forcing shot A strong, heavy delivery but not a drive.

Forehand (delivery) A delivery to the right of the central line in the case of a right-handed player or to the left in the case of the left-handed bowler.

Fours The basic game of bowls as played between two teams each of four players. Also known as **rinks.**

Grass A term used to describe the path or line taken by the bowl in its curved run to the jack. To take or need more grass means to take a wider arc. The description **Green** is also used in this context.

Grassed The point where the bowl leaves the delivering hand and is smoothly grounded to begin its run down the rink.

Green (a) The playing area surrounded by the ditch and bank. This is divided into rinks; or (b) a term used to describe the path or line taken by the curved run of the bowl on its way to the jack. The description **Grass** is also used in this context.

Green-keeper The person responsible for the upkeep and playing condition of the green. Also **Green Manager, Green Ranger, Green Steward.**

Greys Mode of club dress required for the less formal events, comprising grey trousers/skirt and white shirt and jacket.

Grip The manner, of which there are several, of holding the bowl in the hand for the delivery. See **Claw, Cradle** and **Finger** grips.

Guard An alternative term for a block or blocking shot.

Hand The delivering shot, either **Forehand** or **Backhand.**

Head The grouping of live bowls and the jack on the green or carpet after delivery.

Heavy A bowl delivered with too much weight, resulting in the bowl overrunning the intended resting point.

Heavy green A slow green caused probably by rain or over-long grass.

Jack The small white ball used as the target. Other terms, such as **Kitty** and **Cot** are sometimes used locally.

Kill an end The act of causing a dead end by driving the jack over the boundaries of the rink.

Kitty Name for jack, as used in some countries and areas.

Land The amount of green required to aim off in order to counter the action of the bias. This will vary on different greens and under different conditions.

Laying shot The bowl laying closest to the jack or the owner of such a scoring shot.

Laws There are, of course, Laws governing the separate types of bowls played in the British Isles. Those relating to the outdoor Lawn Bowls, to the Indoor game and to the Short-Mat game are reproduced in Appendix I.

Lead The first player in a team game.

Leader As lead.

Length The distance from the mat or the delivering player to the jack, or his settled bowl. Hence 'to be of good length' means that a bowl is lying on a line with the jack.

Line The central point on the rink on to which the jack is centred. If you can combine a perfect length and line your bowl will trickle up to the jack.

Live bowl A correctly delivered bowl which has travelled 15 yards or more from the front of the mat and comes to rest within the confines of the rink and is therefore eligible to score, subject to its position and that of the opposing bowls.

Long jack A jack placed or cast way down the rink and coming to rest probably six to ten feet from the ditch. The jack must be delivered to rest not less than six feet from the rear Ditch, if less than six feet it will be moved back to the six-foot centred position.

Long mat A game played with the mat placed well back towards the minimum distance from the rear ditch and generally with the jack well forward giving a long delivery.

Marker The independent, impartial and experienced person assisting the players in a singles game.

Mat the oblong movable base, usually rubber, from which the delivery, and various measurements, are made. The British mat measures 24 inches long by 14 inches wide and is placed lengthwise down the rink.

Measure (a) The act of measuring the distance of two or more bowls from the jack so as to determine the scoring bowl(s); or (b) a form of measuring instrument. Special bowls measures should be used.

Middle-man The middle or number two player in a triples game.

Narrow The term used for a bowl which has been delivered incorrectly without due regard to the required grass-line or the bias of the bowl. That is, with not enough arc so that the bowl travels too directly to the jack and therefore passes it to the right or left.

Non-toucher A bowl which has finished in the ditch (or rebounded from the bank) without first touching the jack. Such a non-toucher is a dead bowl.

Number three The third member in a fours or rinks game; the deputy skip.

Number two The second player in a triples or fours team having special duties.

Open-hand The side of a head which may happen to offer the best chance of reaching the jack by virtue of the lack of other bowls blocking the path.

Open jack A jack visible from the mat and not blocked by other bowls.

Opening the head The act of moving (by a firing or other heavy shot) a cluster of bowls gathered in front of the jack so that a following player can draw to the jack.

Pace The pace or speed of bowling greens varies from green to green and even on the same green under various conditions. The pace is timed by calculating the number of seconds taken for a bowl to travel 30 yards in a straight line from the mat. Most English greens average about 12 seconds. The pace affects the bias of the bowl.

Pairing The act of matching an opponent's bowl with one of your own. This might be necessary if there is a back wood or other potentially dangerous bowl.

Pairs The game as played between two teams each of two players.

Percentage shot The choice of shot or tactic which has the best chance of turning the head and/or the score to your advantage. Many factors come into deciding the percentage shot and these, of course, vary with each game or head according to how you or your opponent are playing. It is obviously better to go for a shot which has an 80 per cent chance of turning to your advantage than one with only a 20 per cent chance, although sometimes there is much to be said for trying the long-odds shot.

Pitcher A bumper-type delivery where the bowl is badly grassed and is prone to damage the playing surface.

Plant Two (or more) bowls lying close together and in line with the jack or another bowl in such a manner that a blow to the front bowl will push the rear one on to the target.

Point of aim The aiming point chosen to enable the delivered bowl to return to the centre line after the bias has taken effect. In practice, no such visible point or mark is available – it is a question of judgement or trial.

Port A gap in the head through which a bowl may find its way to the jack.

Possession Possession of the rink passes from player to player or from team to team according to whose turn it is to play.

Pulling The act of delivering a narrow bowl by pulling the hand across the body instead of using a straight swing and continuous follow-through.

Rebounding jack Should the jack be driven into the bank and rebound on to the rink (not less than 22 yards from the front of the mat), it remains in play. Similarly, should a jack return to the rink from the ditch due to the action of a toucher, the jack remains in its new position.

Resting A bowl lying against an opposing bowl.

Rink The sub-division of the green on which individual games are played. Green cords separate the individual rinks.

Rinks The basic game played between two teams each of four players. Also known as **Fours.**

Roll-up An informal, friendly game rather than a match or competition.

Rub A bowl diverted from its original path by an intervening bowl.

Running shot A bowl delivered with sufficient weight to overrun the target bowl and perhaps run it out of play into the ditch.

Second The second player in a triples or fours team. Also known as **Number two**.

Semi-fixed stance A stance where the front foot is placed partly down the delivery line before the swing and delivery is begun. The front foot is often then moved further forward to complete the step in the normal way.

Sessions Greens and rinks are normally let out for fixed periods or sessions.

Sets A method of scoring by way of mini-games of say seven points, three or more of these to be played to decide the winner. A form of scoring favoured in televised matches but not officially sanctioned for normal play.

Short A bowl resting short of the jack.

Short end A jack cast to or near the minimum permitted distance. The same objective can be achieved by placing the mat well forward.

Short jack A delivered jack which, when centred, lies at or a few yards past the minimum 25 yards from the centre of the front edge of the mat.

Short mat A game played with the mat placed well forward towards the maximum distance from the rear ditch.

Short-Mat Game A mini-version of the Indoor Bowls game played on a short-length mat and with special rules.

Shot A description used to denote the bowl lying closest to the jack.

Shots down The number of scoring bowls held against a player at any point in a game.

Shots up The number of scoring bowls relating to one player or team at any point in a game.

Shoulder of the green The widest part of the arc formed by the bowl on its curved path to the jack or resting point. This shoulder, not the jack, should be used as the aiming-point. It will normally be some two-thirds of the distance between the mat and the jack.

Singles The game as played between two players.

Skip The skipper or captain of a team.

Skipper See **Skip**.

Skipping The act of controlling the game by the skip or captain.

Skittling The act of destroying the head with a firing shot or drive.

Speed of the green The time in seconds taken by a bowl to travel from delivery to a jack 30 yards down the rink – about 14 seconds on a fast green, 10 seconds or less on a slow one.

Spoon match Semi-friendly club competition where, in most cases, the teams are chosen by lot and small rewards are offered to the winners.

Springing The act of moving a bowl or jack by first hitting another bowl which is lying very near or touching that object. The force will react through the first bowl on to the object bowl or jack.

Stamping of bowls Each bowl should bear an official stamp to show that it has been tested and has a minimum bias. This rule was relaxed in 1986, at least for club, county and national events.

Stance The initial position taken on the mat for the delivery of each bowl. Most bad deliveries arise from a faulty stance. There are several variations to the stance – **Athletic, Crouch, Fixed** or **Semi-fixed.**

String(s) The string or thread used to define the side boundary of the rink.

Swing (of scores) The change of score made by a good shot taking out an opponent's bowl changing, for example, a potential score of four down to one of three up – a swing of seven points.

Take out The action of knocking out, or away, an opposing well-placed bowl or bowls.

Target bowls A version of the game where the jack is replaced by a mat set out in concentric bands like a target. The scoring depends on the lie of your bowl on the target mat. This is sometimes used indoors, or in conjunction with a short mat.

Thin A narrow delivery.

Third man The third player in a fours or rinks game. He also acts as deputy skip.

Thread The string or strong thread used to mark the side boundaries of the rink.

Threesome A game arranged so that three persons (not two teams of three) can be accommodated.

Tie See **Drawn end.**

Tilt As **Cant**, the slight turning from upright of the bowl in the handling during delivery to amend (to some degree) the bias.

Toucher A bowl that has in the course of its initial delivery touched the jack and remained within the side boundaries of the rink. A bowl continuing into the ditch is still a toucher. A toucher is marked with a chalk cross or other mark, which must be removed before the bowl is delivered again.

Trail The action of running the jack forward with a bowl in such a manner that the two keep close together, as opposed to a knock where the jack may be shot forward parting company with the bowl.

Trial end(s) The practice end or ends played before an important game to enable the players to test the green and the conditions of play.

Trickle The last few feet or yards of the bowl's progress at an ever-slowing pace. The speed of the green will affect the length of trickle and therefore the arc.

Triples The game as played between two teams each of three players.

Umpire The experienced adjudicator employed in serious matches to give decisions on points of Law, disputes, measurements, and so forth.

Weight The force, thrust or momentum used in delivering the bowl (or jack) up the rink.

Whip The extra turning arc of a delivered bowl caused by forces such as a strong wind.

White Name for the jack as sometimes used in Scotland.

Whites Mode of dress required for formal matches. White trousers/skirts are required as well as the normal white shirt, jersey or jacket.

Wick A glancing shot off one or more bowls so changing the direction of the newly-delivered bowl.

Wide A bowl which finishes well to one side of the jack or central line.

Wide head The group of bowls at the head spread across, left and right of the jack.

Wobble The erratic running of the bowl after it has left the hand. This not only looks bad but it takes 'way' off the bowl so that it will almost certainly stop short of its target.

Wood(s) A bowl made of a hard, dense wood – lignum vitae. Bowls are not now made of wood but the old term is sometimes still used.

Wresting out One bowl knocking out of position that of an opponent and, one hopes, taking its place.

Wresting shot A heavy delivery which knocks an opponent's bowl from a favourable position and takes its place.

Wrong bias The delivery of a bowl so that it turns away from the jack, not towards it. This is caused simply by holding the bowl the wrong way about. The bias marking must always be on the inside.

Yard-on A shot intentionally delivered with more than normal weight to trail the jack back a yard or more or to knock out of position an opponent's shot bowl. Literally, you should be aiming to rest your bowl a yard further on than for a draw, but usually more weight is required.

Addresses

International Bowling Board
Hon. Secretary: Bede F. O'Brien, PO Box 27, Palm Beach, Queensland 4221, Australia. Tel: 07534-1351

Lawn Bowls: Men
British Isles Bowling Council
Secretary: Colin Vater, 'Bodheulog', Abernant Road, Aberdare, Mid Glamorgan. Tel: Aberdare 873604

English Bowling Association
Secretary: David W. Johnson, Lyndhurst Road, Worthing, W. Sussex, BN11 2AZ. Tel: 0903-820222

Scottish Bowling Association
Secretary: Peter Smith, 50 Wellington Street, Glasgow, G2 6EF

Welsh Bowling Association
Acting Secretary: Alan Williams, 48 Pochin Crescent, Tredegar, NP2 4JS

Irish Bowling Association
Secretary: Jim Barnes, 212 Sicily Park, Belfast, BT10 0AQ

English Bowling Federation
Secretary: John Webb, 62 Frampton Place, Boston, Lincolnshire, PE21 8EL. Tel: 0205-66201

Lawn Bowls: Women
British Isles Women's Bowling Association
Secretary: Mrs. N. Colling, 2 Inghalls Cottages, Ditteridge, Box, Corsham, Wilts. Tel: 0225-742852

English Women's Bowling Association
Secretary: Mrs. N. Colling, 2 Inghalls Cottages, Ditteridge, Box, Corsham, Wilts. Tel: 0225-742852

Scottish Women's Bowling Association
Secretary: Mrs. E. Allan, 55a Esplanade, Greenock, PA16 7SD

Irish Women's Bowling Association
Mrs. D. Sutton, Flat Two, 102, Downview Court, Downview Park West, Belfast

Welsh Women's Bowling Association
Secretary: Miss Linda Parker, Ffrydd Cottage, 2 Ffrydd Road, Knighton, Powys. Tel: 0547-528331

English Women's Bowling Federation
Secretary: Mrs. D.S. Quincey, 18 Thorold Street, Boston, Lincs, PE21 6PH. Tel: 0205-68729

Indoor Bowls: Men
British Isles Indoor Bowling Association
Secretary: Martin Conlin, 8/2 Back Dean, Ravelston Terrace, Edinburgh. Tel: 031-343 3632

English Indoor Bowling Association
Secretary: Bernard Telfer, 290A Barking Road, London, E6 3BA. Tel: 01-470 1237

Scottish Indoor Bowling Association
Secretary: Jim Barclay, 41 Montfode Court, Ardrossan, KA22 7NJ, Ayrshire. Tel: 0294-68372

Welsh Indoor Bowling Association
Secretary: Ray Hill, 1 Brynheulog Street, Port Talbot, W. Glam, SA13 1AF. Tel: 0639-886409

Association of Irish Indoor Bowls
Secretary: William Burrows, 43 Marlborough Park, Central Belfast, B19 6HN. Tel: Belfast 668055

Indoor Bowls: Women
British Isles Women's Indoor Bowls Council
Secretary: Mrs. J.O. Johns, 16 Windsor Crescent, Radyr, Cardiff, Glam. Tel: Radyr 842391

English Women's Indoor Bowling Association
Secretary: Mrs. P. Allison, 8 Oakfield Road, Carterton, Oxford, OX8 3RB. Tel: 0993-841344

Scottish Women's Indoor Bowling Association
Secretary: Mrs. R. Thompson, 1 Underwood Road, Burnside, Rutherglen, Glasgow, G73 3TE

Welsh Women's Indoor Bowling Association
Secretary: Mrs. Hazel King, Hillcrest Villa, Tynewydd, Treorchy, Rhondda, Mid Glamorgan, CS42 5LU. Tel: 0443-77168

Irish Women's Indoor Bowling Association
Secretary: Mrs. Hazel Getty, 25 Knutsford Drive, Belfast, Northern Ireland. Tel: Belfast 741678

Short-Mat Bowls
English Short-Mat Bowling Association
Secretary: Harry Lockett, 47 Mullion Grove, Padgate, Warrington, Cheshire

Wales and British Isles Short Green Association
Secretary: Ken Dorrington, 8 Clydrach Road, Tonypandy, Rhondda, CF40 2QD
Scottish Secretary: Robert Meiklejohn, 6 Lochalsh Drive, Foxbar, Paisley, PA2 9BY
Irish Secretary: Ronnie McDermott, 77 Cherry Valley Park West, Belfast, BT5 6PU

Magazines
World Bowls
Geoffrey K. Browne, PO Box 17, East Horsley, Surrey, KT24 5JU. Tel: 0372-59319

Bowls International
Key Publishing Ltd, PO Box 100, Stamford, Lincolnshire, PE9 1QX. Tel: 0780-55131

Other addresses
Worthing Bowling Club
Beach House Park, Worthing, West Sussex
Worthing Bowls Centre
33 Brighton Road, Worthing, BN11 3EF.
Bournanza Holidays
Bill Shipton, 4 Westover Road, Bournemouth, Dorset, BH1 2BY. Tel: 0202-293566
Roy Downing
33 Brighton Road, Worthing, West Sussex

Bibliography

Authors of books on bowling seem strangely averse to mentioning other rival works, or at least extremely few include a Bibliography.

I believe, however, that the new bowler should read as many of these reference books as possible. Many tackle the playing of the game from different viewpoints, and they sometimes give conflicting advice! A few books are like this one, angled at the beginner, but more endeavour to turn the average player into a would-be champion.

You can over the winter months work your way through these and other books. The more recent titles such as *Bowl with Bryant* and some classics such as R.T. Harrison's *How to become a Champion at Bowls,* are available at bookshops or at some specialist sports shops. Other older books may well be out of print, but British readers at least can benefit from our still-excellent public library system. In most cases books on bowling will be found under the reference 796.31. Not all books are expensive, the very useful little handbook *Guidance for New Bowlers* published by the English Bowling Association at Worthing, is still priced at under a pound. Costly or cheap all are good value!

I have here listed the modern books known to me in order of their original date of publication and have added, where applicable, to modern titles their unique ISBN number to ease ordering. By modern, I mean post-war books as these are likely to be available at least in reference or public libraries. For those readers who wish for a very full list of earlier books on bowling I would recommend Godfrey R. Bolsover's excellent book, *Who's Who and Encyclopaedia of Bowls* (Rowland Publishers Ltd, Nottingham, 1959), pages 1248-1251.

The British reader may well find some terms used in these books rather strange because several of these bowling works were written by Australian authors and the British editions have not been translated! The books here listed relate to Lawn Bowls, both outdoors and indoors, not to the Crown Green game.

How to Become a Champion at Bowls
R.T. Harrison
(R.W. Hensell & Sons, Victoria, Australia; 1st edition 1939). 17th edition published in 1983.
ISBN 0.959.7152.0.7.
Know the Game – Bowls, Flat & Crown Green
(E.P. Publishing Ltd, East Ardsley; 1st edition 1953, 2nd edition 1981). ISBN 0.7158.0792.7.
Teach Yourself Bowls James Taylor
(English University Press, 1958).
ISBN 0.3400.5529.4.
Who's Who and Encyclopaedia of Bowls
Godfrey R. Bolsover
(Rowland Publishers Ltd, Nottingham, 1959).
Tackle Bowls This Way
Norman King and C.M. Jones
(Stanley Paul, London, 1959).
Bowls, Technique and Tactics
J. Henkinson and P. Walter
(Allen & Unwin, London, 1960).
Indoor Bowls Arthur Sweeney
(Nicholas Kaye, London, 1966).
The Watney Book of Bowls C.M. Jones

(Queen Anne Press, London, 1967).
Bowls: How To Become a Champion C.M. Jones
(Faber & Faber, London, 1972).
ISBN 0.571.09859.2.
Beginner's Guide To Bowls Cyril Johnson
(Pelham Books, London, 1974).
Encyclopaedia of Bowls
Ken Hawkes and Gerald Lindley
(Hale, London, 1974). ISBN 0.7091.3658.7
The Game of Bowls
Norman King and James Medlycott
(A & C Black Ltd, London, 1975).
ISBN 0.7136.1458.7.
Successful Lawn Bowls from Beginner to Expert in Forty Lessons John Dobbie & Wal Davies
(Pelham Books, London, 1978).
ISBN 0.7207.1033.2.
Championship Bowls Bill Irish
(David & Charles, Newton Abbott, 1979).
ISBN 0.7153.7469.9.
How to Play Bowls James Medlycott
(Hamlyn Publishing Group, London, 1980).
ISBN 0.600.31535.5.

Lawn Bowls, Winning Techniques Jock Jepson (Lansdown Press, Auckland, New Zealand, 1982). ISBN 0.86866.069.8.

In Search of the Resting Toucher Graham Kinney (Greenhouse Publications, Richmond, Victoria, Australia, 1982). ISBN 0.909.104.49.2.

John Snell's Winning Bowls
John Snell with Bill Pritchard
(British edition of Australian original, published by Souvenir Press Ltd, London, 1983).
ISBN 0.285.62584.5.

Successful Lawn Bowls
John Dobbie and Wal Davies
(J.M. Dent, Melbourne, Sydney & London, 1983). This is a revised edition of the book first published by Messrs Thomas Nelson (Australia) Ltd in 1977. ISBN 0.86770.023.8.

Play the Game – Bowls James Medlycott (Hamlyn, 1984). This is a limp-cover version of *How to Play Bowls* (1980).
ISBN 0.600.50016.0.

Bowl with Bryant David Bryant, CBE
(Willow Books – W. Collins, 1984).
ISBN 0.00.218025.1.

English Bowling Association:
Guidance for New Bowlers
(English Bowling Association by arrangement with the late G. Howard. 5th edition).

Bryant on Bowls David Bryant, CBE
(Pelham Books Ltd, London, 1985).
ISBN 0.7207.1539.3.
Works with the same title were published by Cassell in 1966 and 1970.

Laws of the Indoor Game
(English Indoor Bowling Association, London, 1985).

Bowls, The Records Patrick Sullivan
(Guinness Superlatives Ltd, Enfield, 1986).
ISBN 0.85112.414.3.

Rules of Bowls – Level Green and Crown Green
Mark Johnstone
(John Jaques & Sons Ltd, Thornton Heath).

English Bowling Association:
The Laws of the Game
(English Bowling Association; 8th edition 1986).

The Story of Bowls – From Drake to Bryant
edited by Phil Pilley
(Stanley Paul, London, 1987).
ISBN 0.09.166380.6.

The BBC Book of Bowls Keith Phillips
(BBC Publications, London, 1987).
ISBN 0.563.20587.3.

The Daily Telegraph/McCarthy and Stone Bowls Yearbook 1988 edited by Donald Newby
(Telegraph Publications, London, 1987)
ISBN 0.86367.220.5.

Improve Your Bowls Tony Allcock
(Willow Books, Collins, London, 1987).
ISBN 0.00.218271.8.

The English Indoor Bowling Association and also the English Bowling Association issue inexpensive handbooks which should be available from your club.

Index

INDEX